Teaching
for Learning
at University

Teaching and Learning in Higher Education Series
Series Editor: John Stephenson

Teaching
for Learning
at University
Theory and Practice

Denise Chalmers and Richard Fuller

**KOGAN
PAGE**

First published in 1996

Kogan Page Limited
120 Pentonville Road
London N1 9JN

British Library Cataloguing in Publication Data

A CIP record for this book is available from the British Library.

ISBN 0 7494 2041 3

Typeset by Kogan Page
Printed and bound in Great Britain by Biddles Ltd, Guildford and King's Lynn

Contents

Foreword

Teaching for Learning at University is a book that is long overdue. One of the major problems in higher education is the glaring disparity between what teachers preach about quality learning, and what they practise. The aims of higher education institutions, and of those who teach courses within them, are unexceptional, emphasizing high cognitive skills, flexibility in problem solving, social skills and teamwork, creativity, dealing with novelty, and the like. Yet the teaching methods most commonly used, and the means of assessing learning outcomes, simply do not line up with those high-sounding aims.

The remedy is not simply to provide more recipes for teaching and assessment, but to integrate how we teach with how students learn. One of the things that higher educators have not done in their search for quality enhancement is to tackle head-on how students go about their learning. The teacher's main job is twofold: to ensure that the students are provided with teaching and learning activities that require the kinds of learning that are so confidently addressed in the course aims and objectives; and to be able to assert, by information gained from proper assessment tasks, that students have indeed learned as required or the extent to which they have fallen short of desired standards.

The very core of these teaching and learning activities is to activate the learning strategies appropriate to the various stages of learning. These authors refer to several sets of strategies: strategies for acquiring information, strategies for working with information in a way that manifests under-standing, and strategies for confirming learning. These are used at various stages in learning for understanding, and their specific nature depends on the content area being handled. A final set of strategies relates to the students' self-management: strategies for personal management.

The first three sets of strategies have largely been taken for granted by teachers. Good students seem to acquire them naturally, but in the past teachers have not seen it as their job to see that students learn them; their job is to teach content. However, if the hallmark of good teaching is evidence for good learning, and good learning is knowing how to proceed in a content area, then the how of learning is simply the other side of the coin of learning *what*.

This book argues strongly that the *teacher* is indeed the one who is ultimately responsible for the strategies students use. Students will within reason respond to whatever tasks the teacher sets, balanced with a greater or lesser aim to conserve their effort in doing so. Good teaching, then, involves setting up teaching and learning activities that require the appropriate strategies to be used, and the basic content will be learned the better for that. Good teachers, as already good learners in their content areas, themselves know and use these strategies. Chalmers and Fuller simply help them to reflect upon, extract, and apply those skills in their own teaching. Making notes from text, or from lectures, for example, are not detachable skills that can as well be taught by the counselling service or by a study skills expert. The effectiveness of good note-taking depends upon what it is you are taking notes of; and the best judge of that is the teacher, the content expert. These authors have a step-by-step programme that teachers can easily adapt to their own content.

The effectiveness of this work has been established in the authors' own research and in staff development with teachers in quite different teaching areas. It was my privilege a year or so ago to see this work in action at Edith Cowan University, and it is not only theoretically sound: it works. I have no doubt that any teacher who in honesty asks, 'How can I teach to help my students learn more effectively?' will find much food for thought and for productive action in these pages.

John Biggs
Hong Kong, July 1995

Series Editor's Preface

This book by Denise Chalmers and Richard Fuller is a timely addition to the Teaching and Learning in Higher Education Series, offering practical advice within a theoretical framework to teachers concerned with helping students to learn how to learn.

The trend to student-directed learning is gathering pace in higher education. This trend is being stimulated by a number of factors: changes in the workplace, putting a premium on self-reliance, portfolio management and continual updating; pressure on resources and student–staff ratios; wider access; new technology and a broader range of information sources; and keener awareness of the way students achieve a deeper understanding of key concepts.

There have been many curriculum responses to the need to develop greater student autonomy – including those described in earlier books in this Series (eg, *Using Learning Contracts*, *Using Records of Achievement* and *Using Group-Based Learning*). This new book, *Teaching for Learning at University*, meets an equally important need – helping teachers within more conventional course structures to help students to manage their own learning.

Too often, the development of something called 'study skills' is considered to be an extra activity, lacking an integrated strategy for learning and unrelated to main-stream subject teaching. It is easy for discipline-based lecturers to assume that all students are fully proficient in component skills of learning – even basic skills such as taking notes from books and other sources. This book gets down to that kind of detail, while still presenting advice on overall strategies for both the teacher and the learner.

This book will be extremely useful to new and experienced teachers wishing to support students who are learning to learn.

John Stephenson
Director, Higher Education for Capability
Leeds, 1996

Acknowledgements

We have a number of people and organizations we would like to thank for their contribution to our work and to this book.

Special thanks to Denise Kirkpatrick for her contribution to the research projects, teaching programme, and the staff development programme.

Our thanks to the many students at Edith Cowan University who participated in our research projects, and particularly those who were our 'guinea pigs' as we developed and implemented our learning strategies programmes. Their willing participation, enthusiasm, encouragement and constructive criticism were invaluable.

We would like to thank Edith Cowan University and the Australian Research Council which supported our work with a number of research grants (eg, Chalmers, 1994; Chalmers and Fuller, 1994; Chalmers et al., 1992; Fuller et al., 1993). In addition, Edith Cowan University supported us with funding from the Quality Assurance Programme (Chalmers et al., 1994). This enabled us to develop and implement the staff development programme 'Developing a programme to enhance students' learning' with university teachers from different faculties who developed and implemented their own learning strategies programme over one semester.

Our thanks go to the 14 university teachers who participated in the staff development project. Their commitment to teaching and learning meant that they were willing to participate fully in the programme and try out new ways of teaching to improve student learning. Their advice, comments and encouragement to us and to each other made it a wonderful learning opportunity for us all. Specifically, our thanks to: Kevin Barry, Loraine Corrie, Judith Cousins, Fran Cuipryk and Paul Swan from the Faculty of Education; Joseph Emmanuel, Len Therry and Roger Willcocks from the Faculty of Business; Lynne Hunt and Anne Ingamells from the Faculty of Health and Human Sciences; Monica Leggett and Jan Ring from the Faculty of Science and Technology; and Jill Durey and Graham McKay from the Faculty of Arts.

Finally, our thanks to Professor John Biggs for writing the Foreword to this book, and for his contribution to, and encouragement of, our work over a number of years.

Overview

This programme grew out of our work as teachers and researchers. Our teaching experiences made us realize that our students were not always learning in a way that made the subject matter meaningful to them so that it could be applied to their work or life experiences. The students seemed to separate their university knowledge from their common or experiential knowledge. In our research we investigated students' learning goals and their management of learning. Both our teaching and research experiences led us to examine our underlying assumptions and expectations of student learning, and the role of teachers in the learning process. This book is the result of that process.

The book has been written in three separate parts so that it is not necessary to read it from cover to cover. If you would like to know more of the theoretical background and research in the areas of student learning, learning strategies and teaching learning strategies, Part One provides an outline of these. If you want to teach learning strategies to your students, Part Two describes a range of learning strategies and how they can be taught. If you are interested in the experiences of university teachers who have taught a range of learning strategies while teaching subject matter, Part Three describes a staff development programme and case studies of teachers who developed and implemented their own learning strategies programmes. It also provides some guidelines on planning and developing a teaching programme that includes both learning strategies and subject matter.

While you may read only the sections that interest you, we hope that you will find that you want to read the other sections. Reading all of the book will provide you with an overview of why it is important to teach learning strategies in the context of regular course work, as well as why it is necessary to teach them in particular ways. So while each part can be read in isolation, all are linked, with each part informing the others.

Part One, 'Learning and teaching at university', provides an overview of perspectives and research that have guided our research and teaching. It begins by outlining perspectives on learning and teaching, including the goals and purpose of university education, and the quality of student learning

1

and reasons for the type of learning that results. The theoretical perspective on learning that provides the conceptual framework for our book is outlined, as is a framework in which we describe and organize learning strategies. The effects of assessment on learning are examined and recommendations made on using assessment to promote effective learning. Part One concludes with a review of learning and teaching at university and highlights a number of points that should guide university teachers when they develop a learning strategies programme for implementation in their own classes.

Part Two, 'Learning and teaching strategies', describes a range of learning and teaching strategies that can be readily applied in any university class. It includes strategies for acquiring information, working with information, confirming learning, and personal management. Some teaching strategies have been included because they are specifically relevant to the learning strategies described.

Part Three, 'Teaching learning strategies in context', describes a staff development programme developed and implemented with a group of 14 university teachers. It includes five case studies which describe the experiences of some of the teachers who developed their own programmes and taught learning strategies in their own courses. It concludes with recommendations and cautions for developing and implementing a learning strategies programme in your own teaching programme.

We hope that this book provides you with information, ideas and insights on teaching at university. We also hope that you teach some learning strategies in your classes. Please let us know your comments and your experiences. We would appreciate hearing from you.

Denise Chalmers and Richard Fuller can be contacted at University Learning Systems, Edith Cowan University, Goldsworthy Road, Claremont 6010, Western Australia; Tel: +619 442 1495; Fax: +619 442 1483.

Part 1: Learning and teaching at university

Chapter 1:

Perspectives on Learning and Teaching

Goals and purpose of university education

There have been significant changes in policies, organization, staffing, funding and management of universities over a number of years. Many of these changes have occurred as a consequence of government policies and not always with the willing cooperation of the universities concerned. One consequence of these changes is that students who now attend university are no longer drawn from an elite or privileged group but are more heterogeneous and representative of the general population. Both universities and students are adjusting to these changes with varying degrees of success.

While there have been significant changes in almost all aspects of university education, there continues to be general agreement among educators and policy makers about the goals and purpose of higher education. An Australian Government report, for example, states that the major function of university education is to 'increase individuals' capacity to learn, to provide them with a framework with which to analyse problems and to increase their capacity to deal with new information' (Dawkins, 1987, p.1). A subsequent government report suggested that as a result of university education, 'university graduates should possess a capacity to look at problems from a number of different perspectives, to analyse, to gather evidence, to synthesize, and to be flexible, creative thinkers' (Aulich, 1990, p.3). These stated goals are shared with providers of higher education in other Western nations throughout the world.

Few would disagree that these are appropriate goals for higher education, though many would add to them. Edith Cowan University, for example, identifies several characteristics its graduates should possess as outcomes of their university experience:

thinks critically, reasons logically and has well developed problem-solving skills; has good interpersonal skills and is able to work as a member of a team and organization; and has the desire and the skills for continued intellectual development, creativity and enterprise (Edith Cowan University, 1994, p.6).

In common with the characteristics described by Edith Cowan University, the Aulich Report (1990) urged universities to include higher level learning skills in their curriculum so that students would be able to continue learning at the completion of their formal university education. This goal was more fully argued in the recent report for the National Board of Employment, Education and Training which recommended that universities provide undergraduate university students with a range of learning skills and attitudes to enable them to be lifelong learners (Candy *et al.*, 1994).

Not only do the policy makers in government and universities agree on the goals and purpose of higher education; most university teachers have also been found to agree. University teachers from Australia and Canada, for example, agreed that their educational goals were to teach students to analyse ideas or issues critically, develop students' intellectual and thinking skills and teach students to comprehend principles or generalizations (Ramsden, 1992, p.20). A number of university teachers also added that students should have the capacity to respond flexibly to changing circumstances, be able to learn throughout their lifetime, and to integrate theory and practice (Ramsden, 1992).

While these goals were identified by university teachers, they were likely to be expressed as specific goals related to a discipline of study. For example, history teachers wanted their students to demonstrate the effective use of evidence and social awareness, while physics teachers wanted their students to demonstrate the ability to interpret and analyse experimental data (Ramsden, 1992). It is important to note that while the specific goals were discipline-related, they were not directed at the accumulation of knowledge of specific content of a discipline, but at the more general principles of critical thinking and understanding.

While there is general agreement on the goals of universities, it is also clear that many students complete university without achieving these objectives. Dahlgren (1984) reviewed a number of studies on the outcomes of student learning at university and found that final-year students were generally able to reproduce large amounts of factual information, complete complex routine skills and computations, apply algorithms, demonstrate detailed subject knowledge using the appropriate terminology, and pass the set examinations. However, he also found that many students continued to hold misconceptions of important concepts, and were unable to demonstrate that they understood what they had learned, apply their knowledge to a new problem, or work cooperatively to solve problems. As a result of his review, Dahlgren concluded that university students' conceptual changes 'were relatively rare, fragile and context-dependent occurrences' (1984, p.33). A number of more recent studies have confirmed Dahlgren's general findings (Ramsden, 1992).

It would seem that many students complete university without achieving the intended goals of university education. These students achieve only a basic understanding of the discipline they are studying. They are able to recite facts, manipulate the jargon, and survive the assessments, but lack awareness of their own limited understanding of the principles of the discipline (Ramsden, 1992). The ways in which students view and approach their learning, and the ways in which teachers view and approach their teaching may provide some explanation of why students do not achieve the learning that universities claim they provide.

How students view their learning: conceptions of learning

Students begin a course of study with a set of beliefs about the nature of learning and what they intend to achieve (Biggs and Moore, 1993). Beliefs about what learning is and how learning takes place are called 'conceptions of learning'. These are derived from earlier school and learning experiences as well as the students' current goals and motives.

In a study conducted by Säljö (1979), university students were asked to describe what they thought about learning. From these descriptions Säljö identified five different conceptions of learning. A number of subsequent studies have confirmed the same five conceptions (eg, Marton and Ramsden, 1987; Van Rossum and Schenk, 1984), and more recently identified a sixth (Marton, dall'Alba and Beaty, 1993). The six conceptions are:

1. *A quantitative increase in knowledge.* Learning is seen as acquiring information or 'knowing a lot' or 'knowing more'. This acquisition takes place as a result of absorbing and storing knowledge.
2. *Memorizing and reproduction.* Learning is seen as storing information that can be reproduced as isolated pieces of knowledge. This takes place through rote learning, repetition and memorizing.
3. *Applying knowledge.* Learning is seen as acquiring facts, skills or procedures that can be retained and used as necessary. This takes place through the acquisition of knowledge that can be applied or used.
4. *Making sense or abstracting meaning.* Learning is seen as relating parts of the subject matter to other known parts and to the real world. This takes place through relating what is learned to other knowledge.

5. *Interpreting and understanding reality in a different way.* Learning is seen as involving a change in understanding or comprehending the world by re-interpreting knowledge. This takes place when learners identify patterns in information and relate these to information from different contexts and situations. As a consequence of identifying relationships that have not previously been recognized, learners change their understanding in a qualitatively different way.
6. *Changing as a person.* Learning is seen as understanding the world differently and as a consequence learners change within themselves. This takes place through a deep involvement in learning and by being *in charge* of one's learning.

These six conceptions are thought to form a hierarchy, starting at the lowest level at which learning is seen as simply knowing more, through to where learning is seen as changing the person. As a hierarchy, each level encompasses all of the levels below. For example, a student who holds the fifth conception of learning may still see learning as involving memorization and the acquisition of information, but acquires the information for the purpose of understanding the world in a different way.

The first three of these conceptions are usually described as quantitative. Essentially, they relate to *knowing more* and are concerned with acquiring isolated facts, skills or procedures. Generally this learning involves lower level cognitive processes such as rote learning or repetition. The last three conceptions are described as qualitative. They relate to *understanding* and are concerned with understanding the meaning of information and relating new information to what is already known. Generally this learning involves higher level cognitive processes, such as critical analysis and evaluation.

How students approach their learning

Students generally tackle new learning tasks in the same way they tackled previous learning tasks, described as their 'approach to learning' (Biggs, 1987). The approach adopted depends on the students' goals, motives and strategies as well as their interpretation or perception of the demands and requirements of the learning task. Three different approaches have been identified to describe the ways in which students approach their learning: surface, deep and achieving.

Surface approach

The surface approach to learning is based on a principle or intention that is external or extrinsic to the real purpose of the task. This means that the learner's intention is not to understand or learn the information in any lasting way but only to give the impression that learning has taken place, often to obtain marks or complete the task. The strategy based on this approach is to 'satisfice', which involves meeting the task demands with as little time and effort as possible (Biggs, 1993a). Students memorize the subject material as isolated items, without developing any significant understanding of it. What they learn is unlikely to be transferred to new situations and is easily forgotten (Biggs and Moore, 1993). Students who hold quantitative conceptions of learning typically adopt a surface approach when faced with a learning task (Biggs and Moore, 1993; Marton and Säljö, 1984).

Deep approach

The deep approach to learning is based on the principle or intention of engaging in the task on its own terms so that maximum meaning is extracted from it (Biggs, 1993a). The strategies based on this approach vary, but all involve working with the information at high cognitive levels, identifying main ideas and looking for themes or unifying principles. These involve students in the transformation and restructuring of their knowledge to enable them to understand and interpret the material, and to view it from more than one perspective (Biggs, 1987). These students typically achieve higher grades and retain their understanding for a longer time than students who adopt a surface approach (Trigwell and Prosser, 1991; Watkins and Hattie, 1985). Students who hold qualitative conceptions of learning typically adopt a deep approach when faced with a learning task (Biggs and Moore, 1993; Marton and Säljö, 1984).

Achieving approach

The achieving approach to learning is similar to the surface approach because the intention is external to the real purpose of the task (Biggs, 1987). The intention is to achieve high marks for their own sake, not because high marks indicate high levels of learning. The strategies used by students adopting this approach will vary according to the requirements of task. If the reproduction of information is required to earn high marks, the student will use reproduction and recall strategies. If engagement in the task is required to achieve high marks, then the student will use strategies in the same way as students who adopt a deep approach to their learning. The important difference is that students with an achieving approach will employ whatever strategies are seen as necessary to achieve high marks.

These students use a number of organizational strategies to increase their efficiency: for example, their notes are usually neat and well organized, they plan and use study schedules, and they meet assignment and study deadlines (Biggs and Moore, 1993). In itself the use of these strategies is not wrong, and many students would benefit from better organization and the use of conventional study strategies. The problem is that students who adopt an achieving approach use these strategies only to achieve high marks; they are unlikely to engage in class learning activities for the sake of learning. The challenge for teachers is to ensure that in order for these students to achieve high marks, learning and assessment tasks require them to adopt the strategies used by students with a deep learning approach.

It is important to recognize that it is not the particular strategies that are used to learn that indicate the approach or conception of learning, but the purpose or intention of the learner in using them. For example, it can not be assumed that a student who is actively memorizing information has a surface approach to learning. The student may be memorizing in order to be able to remember details that will make it possible to think about the ideas and work with them.

How university teachers view their teaching: conceptions of teaching

Just as students hold beliefs about learning that affect the way they go about their learning, so teachers hold beliefs about the nature of teaching which affect the way they go about their teaching. Samuelowicz and Bain (1992) identified five conceptions of teaching held by university teachers. These are:

1. *Imparting information.* Teaching is seen as a teacher-centred activity which involves imparting the information or knowledge which makes up the subject matter in a one-way process from the teacher to the student. The teacher's aim is for students to know more as a result of the teaching. The teacher's responsibility is to provide the information, the framework and the appropriate examples.
2. *Transmission of knowledge and attitudes to knowledge, within the framework of an academic discipline.* Teaching is seen as a teacher-centred activity with the emphasis on developing the competence of the students so they can deal with the subject matter and apply the concepts. The teacher's aim is for students to know more and be competent users of the knowledge received from the teacher. The teacher's responsibility is to provide the conceptual framework of the subject so that students can readily acquire it.
3. *Facilitating understanding.* Teaching is seen as a teacher-centred activity with the emphasis on getting students to understand the information so they can apply this to new problems both in and outside the discipline. The teacher's aim is for students to be able to apply their knowledge and understanding in new circumstances. The teacher's responsibility is to make this understanding possible by pitching explanations at the right level.

4. *Activity aimed at changing students' conceptions or understanding of the world.*
Teaching is seen as a cooperative activity, with the student as the less
experienced learner. The teacher's aim is to change students' naive
understandings so that they become more like experts, within the
conceptual framework of the discipline. The teacher's responsibility is
to involve the students actively in their own learning by using a variety
of teaching strategies and methods to achieve that end.

5. *Supporting student learning.* Teaching is seen as a student-centred activity
in which students are responsible for their learning and the content of
that learning. The teacher's aim is to encourage and sustain the students'
own interests. The teacher's responsibility is to help plan, monitor and
provide feedback on students' work as well as provide conceptual
guidance. This conception usually applies at the postgraduate level.

These conceptions are seen as increasing in sophistication, with each conception being qualitatively different to the one preceding it. Unlike the conceptions of learning, they are not considered hierarchical but are ordered on a
continuum (Samuelowicz and Bain, 1992). For example, a teacher who holds
the highest level conception of teaching as supporting student learning does
not also hold the lowest level conception of imparting information.

The first three conceptions of teaching are essentially quantitative. The
main focus of teaching is to increase students' knowledge. Teaching involves
the transmission of the knowledge or subject matter that originates from an
external source (Biggs and Moore, 1993). The teacher is seen as central to the
learning process, controlling what is learned, when it is learned and how it is
learned.

The final two conceptions of teaching are essentially qualitative. The main
focus of teaching is to change the way students see and use the knowledge
they have. Teaching involves the facilitation of learning that engages both the
teacher and student in a cooperative activity in order to develop students'
understanding and ways of interpreting the world.

How teachers approach their teaching

Just as students' conceptions of learning are reflected in their approaches to
learning, so too are teachers' conceptions of teaching reflected in their approaches to teaching.

Transmission approach

The transmission approach to teaching is based on the principle or intention
of transmitting knowledge, skills, and procedures from the teacher to the
students. Classes are conducted as information-giving sessions with little
opportunity for student activity. The purpose of the class session is for the

teacher to present the subject matter clearly and accurately. The learning of the information is the responsibility of the students and this is expected to be undertaken in the students' own time. If application tasks are set by the teacher it is to enable students to demonstrate accurate application of the information they have learned. Student learning is assessed by determining how much, and how accurately, information is known, rather than what is understood (Gow and Kember, 1993; Samuelowicz and Bain, 1992). Multiple choice tests, short answer responses and comprehension tasks are commonly used as means of assessment.

Two-way cooperative approach

The two-way cooperative approach to teaching is based on the principle or intention of facilitating student learning through helping students develop problem-solving skills and critical thinking abilities. The teacher uses the students' existing understanding and knowledge as the starting point of the teaching process. The teacher presents subject matter as a way to introduce concepts and processes. The teacher is less central to the teaching process, so classes are usually interactive and group oriented. Teaching activities are selected from a range of alternative methods for the purpose of leading the students to construct their own knowledge, make their own sense of reality, and adopt a conceptual framework in line with that shared by the experts in the field. Teachers adopting this approach hold that an important part of their role is to provide motivation and to stimulate the students' interest (Gow and Kember, 1993; Samuelowicz and Bain, 1992). Student learning is assessed by determining what is understood rather than what is known. Extended response essays, case studies and problem-solving tasks are commonly used as means of assessment.

Implications of conceptions of learning and teaching for the roles of teachers and students

The conceptions of learning and teaching held by teachers and students affect their view of their own role in the learning process. A student who holds the view of learning as knowing more will see the role of the learner and the teacher differently from a student who views learning as understanding the world in new ways. Similarly, a teacher who views teaching as a process of transmission will see the students' role in the learning process differently from a teacher who views teaching as supporting student learning. Therefore, the roles and responsibilities of both students and teachers in the learning process should be clarified.

The practice of separating the roles and responsibilities of the student and the teacher reinforces a common misconception – that teaching is something that occurs at one end of the room under the control of the teacher, and that learning takes place at the opposite end of the room under the control of the students (Gleason, 1985). For example, teachers who focus exclusively on their role as teacher and transmitter of knowledge may use teaching strategies that have a lot to do with transmitting knowledge but little to do with learning. Conversely, students who focus exclusively on the student role as receiver of knowledge will not actively seek new knowledge or under-standing but will learn only what the teacher provides. In the first example, the teacher holds the students accountable for their learning; in the second, students hold the teacher accountable for their learning. Neither view is likely to lead to learning for understanding.

A more desirable view is for the teacher and student to share responsibility for both teaching and learning. This view is held when teachers and students both hold qualitative conceptions of teaching and learning, and see the role of the teacher and students as cooperative and facilitative.

A difficulty occurs when there is a mismatch between the teachers' and the students' conceptions of teaching and learning. This problem is not easily addressed. Teachers who view their role as facilitating student learning and conduct their classes accordingly may arouse resentment in students who see the teachers' role as transmitting information. Conversely, students who see their role as active participants in their own learning may resent a teacher who simply transmits information.

In every class there will be a range of conceptions of learning held by the students. Rather than allowing it to be a problem, teachers can address the differences positively by challenging all students to examine their approach to learning. As university teachers our goals are for students to achieve a full understanding of the subject matter and to be able to assess and analyse ideas critically. Teachers who use teaching strategies to promote a deep learning approach are more likely to achieve these goals than teachers who simply transmit information.

The ways in which students view and approach their learning, and the ways in which teachers view and approach their teaching, provide one explanation of why students do not achieve the intended goals of university learning. Students do not always engage fully in the learning process and may take short-cuts in order to meet course requirements with a minimum of effort. Teachers may encourage this by their use of teaching and assessment methods which focus on quantitative increases in knowledge.

There is another reason why students do not learn at university as effec-tively as we would expect them to do. Teachers often comment that students enter university with few of the relevant learning strategies and skills that enable them to make optimum use of the learning opportunities available to them, as illustrated by the following comment:

It was clear to me that many of the problems students have in learning psychology courses were not so much problems of lack of effort as they were problems of lack of skills in reading, learning from lectures, and learning from other students in discussion classes and in interactions outside class. (McKeachie *et al.*, 1984, p.2)

The students' apparent lack of appropriate learning strategies may be a result of the ways in which schools operate. In secondary schools the teacher usually controls the content of the lessons, the work set for homework, and the monitoring and evaluation of students' work. The teaching focus is on the subject matter rather than the skills involved in learning. Teachers may set a range of activities which incorporate many effective learning strategies, but they are typically not discussed or made a direct focus of instruction (McKeachie *et al.*, 1984). School students may acquire effective learning skills and strategies but this usually happens by chance rather than as a consequence of the instruction they have received. As a result, these students are unlikely to be aware of the learning strategies they do use, and how and in what situations they can be successfully applied.

Another reason why students do not always learn appropriate strategies arises from the type of learning required for school and university entrance examinations. Much of the learning at school requires students to reproduce information provided by the teachers (Cooper, 1994). Some of this information is learned by students imitating the teachers' examples and applying the model to a series of similar examples. For instance, in mathematics, students apply an algorithm they have learned to a number of maths exercises. The students are then tested on the information they have learnt, with those who accurately reproduce the information receiving high marks. One student explains the system: 'Schools teach you to imitate. If you don't imitate what the teacher wants, you get a bad grade' (Pirsig in Ramsden, 1992, p.62). As a consequence of school systems such as these, school students may not actually need to use effective learning strategies. They are able to complete secondary school successfully because of the type of learning required and the learning support provided by teachers.

From such a supportive school system, students come into the university system where they must select appropriate courses, evaluate and monitor their own progress based on varying amounts of feedback and infrequent assessments, and maintain motivation over relatively long periods. University students often have limited contact with academic and general staff and, as a consequence, tend not to receive ongoing and consistent information and advice. Because of this, students are often unaware of the range of support services that are available to them and are not skilled at identifying resources that might assist them during their studies.

While the preceding discussion raises a number of differences between school and university learning, it is not intended to imply that students who enter university from school are ineffective learners. Students enter university with a range of skills and experiences that were appropriate and effective for school learning. However, little of this experience and few of their learning strategies and skills may be appropriate for learning in the university context (Raaheim, 1984).

Addressing the learning needs of students

Students do not come to university fully equipped with the wide range of learning strategies and skills necessary for learning at university. Many leave university after a number of years with inappropriate understanding and ineffective learning strategies and skills (Dahlgren, 1984; Pressley, El-Dinary and Brown, 1992). Educators have tended to assume that students will develop effective learning and study strategies as they grow older and have more experience in learning situations. This assumption is clearly not supported by research and anecdotal evidence (Gaskins and Elliot, 1991; Pressley and McCormick, 1995; Snyder and Pressley, 1990). If students are to develop the ability to think critically and to reason logically, creatively and flexibly in a variety of new situations, university teachers need to examine how and what they teach.

Instead of assuming or hoping that students will mature and develop appropriate strategies, it is better to teach them learning strategies and skills that they can use to learn the subject matter. This is not simply a matter of teaching more, or adding more to the curriculum. Teaching learning strategies involves a change in the way teachers think about teaching. Teachers can help students develop learning and thinking abilities at the same time as they teach subject matter by adjusting the ways in which they teach (McKeachie, 1987).

If students are to learn desired outcomes in a reasonably effective manner, then the teacher's fundamental task is to get students to engage in learning activities that are likely to result in their achieving those outcomes. (Shuell, 1986, p.429)

Chapter 2:

Theoretical Framework of Learning

The theoretical position that guides our understanding of learning and the role of teaching in the learning process has been influenced by the information processing model of thinking and learning.

The information processing model provides an explanation of the cognitive processes involved in learning, and grew from the work of a number of theorists (eg, Atkinson and Shiffrin, 1968; Farnham-Diggory, 1972; Gagné, 1985; Lindsay and Norman, 1977). The model uses the analogy of the human mind as a computer, and uses computer terminology to describe the ways in which people learn from their environment. The environment is the world that contains all the possible information, experiences and interactions available to the learner. A simple illustration of the model is shown in Figure 2.1.

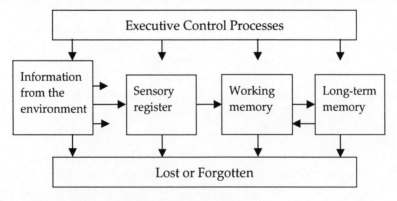

Figure 2.1 *A simple information processing model*

Information processing

Information processing begins by registering information from the environment. This is registered in the sensory register by some, or all, of the senses (touch, sight, sound, smell, taste). However, the sensory register is not like a camera that takes a photograph and records all details. Some of the information is not registered at all, some is ignored and some is simply forgotten. Only a small proportion of information from the sensory register is received by the working or conscious memory. The working memory has only a limited capacity so the information must be processed immediately or it will be forgotten. The most common way of retaining information for immediate or short term use is rehearsal. A common rehearsal strategy is to repeat a telephone number until the number is dialled or written down.

Much of the information that registers in the working memory is immediately forgotten. Forgetting from the working memory is a very useful part of processing information. No one needs to, or even wants to, remember every telephone number they have ever dialled, every car registration number they have ever seen, or every newspaper they have ever read. However, it can be very frustrating when important things are forgotten: for example, failing to remember the registration number of a car involved in an accident, or the new telephone number of a friend.

For information to be retained longer than a few seconds, it must be actively processed and stored in the long-term memory. The processes that enable information to be stored in, and recalled from, the long-term memory are encoding, storage and retrieval. Encoding is the process of transferring information from the working memory to the long-term memory so that it is ready to be stored. Storage is the process of linking and placing information in structures or memory stores. Retrieval is the process of locating and recalling information to the working memory.

The long-term memory is not directly open for conscious inspection. Thinking is carried out in the working or conscious memory. Both new information from the environment and old information from the long-term memory are encoded, stored and retrieved in a constant exchange between the working and long-term memory. The cognitive processes involved in adding new information to old information, and re-examining old information in the light of new information, are generally referred to as 'processing information'. The more that information is processed, the more usable and accessible it is to the person.

The processes involved in transferring information from the environment to the long-term memory are guided and directed by a number of executive control processes. These include directing attention, selecting strategies, monitoring progress towards goals, and motives. The executive processes determine what information the person will take from the environment, whether it is processed in the working memory, whether and how it is encoded, where and with what other information it is stored, and when and why it is retrieved. It is at this executive level where processing and thinking differ most for each person. This explains why two people can witness the same event and recall it in totally different ways. Each person constructs his/her own memory of the event. The information that is first processed may differ depending on where attention was directed and what was important to each person.

Learning involves the construction of information in the memory, rather than the exact transmission of information directly from the environment to the memory of the learner. The ways in which learners actively acquire and manipulate information from the environment and their memory involve the use of learning or cognitive strategies. These strategies are a collection of tactics that enable the individual to acquire knowledge and skills: for example, reading for understanding and memorizing information.

Strategies may be used consciously or unconsciously. Children learn how to read without being consciously aware of the cognitive strategies they are using. This lack of conscious awareness is not a problem until different types of reading are required. For example, reading for key ideas is different from reading for enjoyment, and different from skim reading to identify the main idea. Students who are unaware of these different strategies are unable to use them in situations when they are needed. Awareness of cognitive strategies, and being able to use strategies when and where they should be used, are important metacognitive aspects of thinking and learning.

Metacognition and types of knowledge

The term 'metacognition' is used to refer to two aspects of thinking: the first refers to the awareness of, and knowledge about, cognition; the second relates to the control and regulation of cognition (Brown *et al.*, 1983; Campione *et al.*, 1989).

The awareness aspect of metacognition relates to the learners' conscious knowledge of their own thinking processes and of themselves as learners. For example, learners may know that they can remember names and faces easily, that they can write well or understand quickly. Awareness also relates to their knowledge of the various learning strategies that they could use, and how to use them to meet the demands of a particular learning task (Campione *et al.*, 1989). Another aspect of metacognitive awareness is the learners' perceptions of their competence and self-concept (McKeachie *et al.*, 1987).

These awareness and knowledge aspects of metacognition are often referred to as declarative, procedural and conditional knowledge (Paris *et al.*, 1983). It is useful to outline these more fully so that the instructional process addresses all three types of knowledge.

Declarative knowledge refers to *knowing that*. This term covers what is commonly referred to as 'knowledge', and includes facts, beliefs, theories, opinions, values, rules, names, and so on. It is often knowledge isolated from the learner's personal experience (Biggs and Moore, 1993), such as knowledge learned at school or from the media, but it can also be derived from the learners' own experiences.

Procedural knowledge refers to *knowing how*, and generally involves some sort of action. Often both declarative and procedural knowledge are involved when carrying out an action. For example, knowing and being able to state the rules for calculating a multiplication solution involves declarative knowledge, but being able to calculate and solve the multiplication problem involves procedural knowledge.

Conditional knowledge refers to *knowing when and why*; it involves knowing when declarative and procedural knowledge should be used, and applying them strategically. Conditional knowledge is used when one procedure is used before another in order to complete the task effectively. For example, conditional knowledge is evident when a student uses a skim reading strategy to scan for relevant information from a textbook, and then uses a focused reading strategy when studying for a test.

Although the awareness of and knowledge about cognition is an important aspect of metacognition, it is the second aspect of metacognition, involving the control and regulation of cognition, that is more important (McKeachie *et al.*, 1987). This is because this aspect controls and regulates the use of strategies that are known by the learner.

These control and regulation aspects of metacognition include three general processes: planning, monitoring, and self-regulation or checking. These three processes are responsible for directing, regulating and overseeing learning (Brown *et al.*, 1983).

Planning activities are usually undertaken before beginning a problem or task and include setting goals, predicting outcomes, scheduling the order in which particular strategies are to be used, and carrying out various forms of trial and error simulations to anticipate errors and problems. These activities help learners decide which strategies to use and how to process information effectively. They also help learners recall any relevant knowledge from the long-term memory which makes organizing and comprehending the information easier.

Monitoring activities are an essential aspect of regulation and include testing, revising, and rescheduling or reorganizing strategies when the learner is actually involved in the learning task. Monitoring is involved when learners track their attention while reading and carry out self-testing while reading a text to check their comprehension. These various monitoring activities help learners understand the information and integrate it with their existing knowledge (McKeachie *et al.*, 1987).

Self-regulation involves evaluating the outcome of the learning task against criteria or goals for efficiency and effectiveness (Brown *et al.*, 1983). Examples of these activities include adjusting the speed of reading in response to the difficulty of the text, reviewing information to check for comprehension, and using test-taking strategies such as skipping questions that are too difficult. These self-regulating activities have been shown to improve learning performance by helping learners check and correct their behaviour as they work through a task (Campione *et al.*, 1989).

Generally, the awareness aspect of metacognition is fairly stable. Learners' knowledge about their ability to remember details, for example, is unlikely to change according to different learning tasks or situations. However, this knowledge may not be accurate, and learners may consider that they are able to remember easily, or to write well, when they cannot. On the other hand, the self-regulation aspect of metacognition is susceptible to change as it is task- and situation-dependent (Brown *et al.*, 1983). For example, planning, monitoring and self-regulation activities would vary considerably when researching for an assignment compared to preparing for a weekend holiday.

Constructivism

At a broader level this theoretical framework can be considered to be constructivist in nature. Essentially, constructivism emphasizes that people construct knowledge for themselves as a result of their interactions with their environment. Through this construction process, individuals build their own understandings and ways of looking at the world (Biggs, 1993b). This does not mean that each person constructs knowledge and understanding in a totally different way from others. Knowledge and understanding are constructed in an agreed and shared social context. The qualitative conceptions of learning and teaching are encompassed by the constructivist view of learning.

Constructivism subsumes a variety of theories, including information processing and social cognitive theories. The main theorists who can be included under this framework are Gagné (1985), Piaget (1950), Sternberg (1983; 1985), Vygotsky (1978), and the metacognitive theorists (Brown and Campione, 1990; Brown *et al.*, 1983).

Implications for teaching: from theory to practice

The constructivist views of learning are important because they inform teachers of where they can best direct their teaching activities in order to promote effective learning. According to this viewpoint, the important features of thinking include the basic cognitive processes of encoding, storage and retrieval, strategies to guide those processes, knowledge about those strategies and one's own thinking processes, knowledge about the world in general, motivational beliefs, goals and overall cognitive style (Snyder and Pressley, 1990). All of these interact with each other, facilitating, directing, guiding and monitoring learning. This view of learning addresses the cognitive, metacognitive, and social-emotional aspects of thinking. If teachers direct their teaching at these aspects of the learning process, they are more likely to help their students use effective learning processes and strategies.

The immediate implications for teaching are that teaching strategies need to be directed firstly at students' encoding of information so that they remember and associate it with other information, secondly at the ways in which students work with the information to promote understanding, and thirdly at the way in which students demonstrate their learning. The immediate implications for learning are that students must be active learners and must be able to use a variety of learning strategies that will help them learn with understanding. Teachers can help students do this by explicitly teaching them about learning strategies, and by encouraging students to use them appropriately.

Identifying learning strategies

Learning strategies have been described as a collection of cognitive or mental tactics that are used by an individual in a particular learning situation to facilitate learning (Derry and Murphy, 1986). For example, a student who reads and re-reads a chapter in a textbook is using a simple type of strategy to learn the subject matter. A student who asks him or herself questions about the subject matter and writes answers to these questions is using a more complex learning strategy. The first strategy is likely to result in the student remembering the information, while the second is likely to result in the student understanding the information.

McKeachie *et al.* (1987) developed a taxonomy of learning strategies that describes the range of strategies needed for effective learning at university. They are grouped into three broad categories: cognitive, metacognitive, and resource management. The cognitive category includes strategies related to the learning and understanding of information. The metacognitive category includes strategies that involve planning, regulating, monitoring, and modifying cognitive processes. The resource management category includes strategies that control resources (time, effort, support) which influence the students' involvement in the learning task.

Cognitive strategies

Cognitive strategies involve rehearsal, elaboration and organization. These strategies enable the learner to encode, store and retrieve information and relate it to the basic cognitive processes of learning.

Rehearsal strategies are used to encode information in order to learn and reproduce information exactly as it is presented. Examples include reciting lists, repeating a task such as multiplication tables or a music score over and over, copying material verbatim, note taking and underlining text.

Elaboration strategies are used to increase the connections between new information and what is already known. The aim is to increase the meaningfulness of the information. A basic elaboration strategy is the use of a mnemonic such as the rhyme 'Thirty days hath September...' to help us remember the number of days in each month. More complex elaboration strategies include paraphrasing, summarizing, and creating analogies.

Organizational strategies are used to structure information so that it is encoded and stored with related information. Examples include outlining the main ideas and generating hierarchies, charts and tables.

Metacognitive strategies

As indicated earlier, metacognition is concerned with knowledge about cognition, and the control and regulation of cognition. The taxonomy focuses on the control and self-regulation aspects of metacognition, and includes planning, monitoring and self-regulation strategies.

Planning strategies include identifying and setting goals, and then formulating a plan of action to achieve the goals. This involves selecting strategies that are likely to be effective in reaching these goals. For example, learners may choose to skim read in order to gain an overview of a topic, and then to generate their own questions to guide learning of that topic.

Monitoring strategies include testing, revising, rescheduling and reorganizing while actually involved in the learning task. These strategies help the learner stay focused on the learning goal while working through the learning task. Monitoring strategies may include self-testing, checking the focus of attention, and test-taking strategies.

Regulating strategies are used when monitoring indicates that some changes should be made to the learning process. For example, learners who realize that they are not understanding what they are reading might decide to adjust their reading rate or re-read and review the materials.

Resource management strategies

Resource management strategies help students manage their environment and available resources. These include the time available for study, the actual study environment, and the support of others in the learning situation, such as teachers and peers. McKeachie *et al.* (1987) also include personal management of effort, persistence and mood. While these could be included with cognitive or metacognitive strategies, they were thought to be different enough to be categorized separately. Sternberg (1985) also identified resource strategies as important since they enable learners to adapt to the environment and to change the environment to fit their needs.

Time management is an important self-management strategy and is a traditional component of study skills programmes. Time management includes semester, monthly and weekly planning, as well as the management of time within an individual study session. It also involves setting goals, identifying priorities and flexibly managing time to achieve them.

Study environment management involves students in identifying the physical conditions under which they work best and adapting their environment to meet these conditions. This may involve setting up a study desk in a quiet, well-lit corner of the house where distractions can be minimized. If it is not possible for students to adapt or find a suitable environment then they must locate a place where their requirements can be met. This may mean working in the university library, in student study rooms, or in a quiet courtyard. The location itself is not important. What is important is that students organize their study environment so that they can focus their attention on their study.

Effort management relates to students' personal motivations, persistence and attributions for their performance. The most important aspect of these is how students manage the effort they put into a task. Students need to know when it is worth increasing their effort, and when they should decrease it. Another aspect of effort management is students' attributions for success and failure. It is better if students attribute success to their personal efforts rather than to some outside agency such as the teacher's skill, or luck in getting easy examination questions. If students attribute success to personal effort, they are more likely to increase their effort in order to cope with more difficult aspects of a task. Students can learn strategies that help them attribute success to effort rather than luck or ability. This will help them maintain commitment to the task.

Strategies to manage the support of others involve students knowing where, when and how to seek help from others. In a university context this usually involves teachers and peers, but it may also include academic and support staff. Teachers may welcome the opportunity to work with students on an individual basis, but students need to develop strategies to initiate the contact. In the same way, peer tutoring and peer interactions are a valuable source of, and support for, reciprocal learning, but students are not always skilled at initiating these interactions. Students also need to know about other types of support that are available to them. These include student support services, such as academic skills and career advisers, counsellors and housing officers. Support may also be obtained through access to student union services such as medical advice and grievance procedures. Another source of support available within the faculties is from people such as heads of department, administrative officers, course coordinators and the like. Many students leave university without ever having used these services or becoming aware of their existence. Students need to develop strategies so that they learn to recognize that they do not know something, and can identify someone who is able to provide the appropriate assistance.

Practical skills strategies

The cognitive and metacognitive strategies sections of the McKeachie *et al.* (1987) taxonomy focus on strategies that facilitate the learning of declarative knowledge (knowing what) and conditional knowledge (knowing when and why), but do not include strategies that facilitate procedural knowledge (knowing how). Some disciplines may require strategies that facilitate the demonstration and application of knowledge in a practical way, such as the skills required in computing, science, nursing, and sporting disciplines. If these skills are necessary, then a new category of strategies may need to be added to the taxonomy.

McKeachie *et al.*'s (1987) taxonomy of learning strategies provides one of the most comprehensive classifications of learning strategies. Other more limited classifications were developed by Weinstein and Meyer (1986), Nisbet and Shucksmith (1986) and Dansereau (1985).

Task-focused learning strategies

Learning at university requires students to coordinate their use of the various learning strategies. For example, students who are learning from a textbook have to identify the main points, find examples of these points, and remember and understand the information. As they are reading, they have to monitor their understanding, perhaps re-read various sections of the text and eventually decide when they have learned enough for their purpose. Students rarely use only one strategy at a time. Accordingly, it is more informative for students and teachers if learning strategies are considered in terms of the tasks for which they are used, rather than in terms of separate component strategies. This task-focused classification of learning strategies more adequately fits the definition of learning strategies as a collection of cognitive tactics used to complete a particular learning task. In developing this classification, a number of learning tasks commonly undertaken at university have been identified, and the learning processes and underlying strategies that are needed to complete these tasks in a way that achieves effective learning have been determined. Each task-focused learning strategy includes a number of strategies from the various taxonomy categories identified by McKeachie *et al.* (1987). The single strategies identified by the other classifications form the basic components that together represent a task-focused learning strategy.

The task-focused learning strategies are organized under four categories to represent different learning purposes. These are strategies for acquiring information, working with information, confirming learning, and personal management.

Strategies for *acquiring information* are specifically directed at increasing the knowledge of the learner. The purpose of these strategies is to facilitate the learners' acquisition of a substantial knowledge base so that it can to lead to understanding. While there can be knowledge without understanding, there cannot be understanding without knowledge. The aim is to help students organize information so that what they already know links with the information they need to learn, as well as to develop a knowledge base that is structured within the conceptual framework of the subject discipline. Strategies for acquiring information included in Part Two of this book are skim reading, note making from text and lectures, note making for assignments, identifying main points, memorizing, and accessing information. The task-focused strategies in this category involve many of the cognitive strategies such as rehearsal, elaborating and organizing, as well as the metacognitive strategies of planning, monitoring and self-regulation identified in the McKeachie *et al.* (1987) taxonomy.

Strategies for *working with information* are specifically directed at learners working with information they have acquired in order to understand that information. These strategies are directed at tasks learners need to carry out in order to understand the ideas contained in the information they have acquired. The strategies for working with information provide ways in which students can think about what they have learned and identify underlying principles and associations. Strategies for working with information in Part Two include organizing ideas, making concept maps, asking questions, writing paragraphs, explaining ideas, making summaries from notes, using study groups and using a systematic approach to their learning. Again, they include both cognitive and metacognitive strategies as well as some resource management strategies identified in the McKeachie *et al.* (1987) taxonomy.

Strategies for *confirming learning* are specifically directed at confirming that learning has taken place. These strategies are directed at formal and informal assessment tasks, as well as tasks generated by the learners themselves, such as quizzes and review questions to confirm their own learning. The strategies included in Part Two relate specifically to formal assessment tasks such as preparing for examinations, analysing a question, preparing an assignment, and learning from the feedback given on formal assessments. The strategies included in this category involve cognitive, metacognitive and resource management strategies.

Strategies for *personal management* are specifically directed at learners' personal study management. They incorporate some of the resource management strategies identified by the McKeachie *et al.* (1987) taxonomy. The strategies for personal management included in Part Two include coping with the student role, and study and time management.

While there may be other strategies that could be included in the various categories, the task-focused strategies in Part Two include a range of common tasks that students at university are likely to encounter. One advantage of describing learning strategies in terms of the tasks in which they are located is that it becomes easier for university teachers to determine when students might need help using the various strategies. It also makes it more likely that students will see these strategies as relevant to their learning needs.

Chapter 3:

Teaching Learning Strategies

Review of learning strategies programmes

It is strange that we expect students to learn but seldom teach them about learning. We expect students to solve problems yet seldom teach them about problem solving. And similarly, we sometimes require students to remember a considerable body of material yet seldom teach them the art of memory. (Norman, 1982)

The constructivist viewpoint is a relatively new way of looking at learning and has attracted a great deal of interest and research, particularly over the last two decades. Two extensive reviews of this research on learning, and the role of teaching in the learning process were conducted by Derry and Murphy (1986) and Pressley and McCormick (1995). Much of this research was carried out with primary and high school students; little was specifically carried out in a university context. Because of the paucity of university based research, principles derived from the school based research have been extracted and applied to the university context. The few studies that have been carried out in universities are referred to whenever possible. The reviews of this research identify that the effectiveness of any programme designed to teach learning strategies depends on the learning context, the control of instruction, and the information provided at the time of instruction.

The context of learning strategy instruction

Learning strategies and skills can be taught either as a separate subject or integrated so that the content of existing courses and the learning strategies relevant to learning the content are taught together. Both separate and integrated learning strategy programmes have particular strengths and problems. A summary of these strengths and problems is presented in order to identify the most effective context in which a learning strategies programme should be taught.

Separate learning strategies programmes

Some universities offer courses that teach students about learning strategies. These are usually intended to be relevant to students regardless of subject areas. Programmes that teach learning strategies in this way are known as separate learning strategies programmes. Such programmes treat subject matter as incidental material in which the learning strategies can be practised (Derry and Murphy, 1986). These programmes include instruction in a range of learning, general processing and self-management strategies as well as opportunities to apply them. The specific strategies are selected because they are considered to be applicable to a wide range of learning contexts and tasks. Learning strategy programmes developed by Dansereau (1985) and Weinstein (1982; 1988) are examples of courses that separate the teaching of learning strategies from the teaching of subject matter.

There are a number of problems with separate learning strategies programmes. One is that they decontextualize the learning of the strategies from the learning of subject matter. Another is that they are often based on a deficit view of students: that students lack the required learning skills and therefore need to receive remediation.

Decontextualized learning strategy programmes or study skills courses, such as those developed by Dansereau and Weinstein, have been found to be effective in the short term, with immediate improvements observed in the use of some learning strategies such as study management and note taking strategies. However, longer-term improvement and sustained use of learning strategies, particularly higher level strategies, have not eventuated. It seems that a separate programme does not supply a realistic context for varied practice in strategy formulation and application. Students do not always apply strategies they have learnt to other contexts, because they are unaware that they are relevant to the task. It may be that even when they recognize that a particular strategy is relevant, they do not know how to apply it.

Students need to apply learning strategies to real learning tasks that require them to identify the purpose and goals of the task, and then select strategies that will engage them in activities which will help them achieve their learning goals. The effective use of learning strategies requires sustained practice and application. This is unlikely to happen when the instruction in learning strategies is separated from the context in which those strategies need to be used.

An unintended outcome of separate learning strategy programmes arises when students treat the information on learning strategies as content or information to be learned in the same way that they learn subject matter in other courses. For example, they may focus on learning about the strategy (declarative knowledge) but may overlook the importance of learning how and when to use it (procedural and conditional knowledge).

The second problem associated with separate learning strategies programmes is that they can lead to a perception that students are deficient in learning strategies and therefore need to receive remedial help. In other words, the student does not know how to learn, therefore the student should be 'fixed'. A frequently prescribed remedy to 'fix' students involves improving their learning and study skills. Often a specialist academic skill adviser is called on to provide remedial assistance to students identified as being deficient in learning skills. Students are expected to attend the remedial programmes in their own time. Such programmes have traditionally tried to teach these unsuccessful students to use learning and study strategies as skilfully as successful students (Cloete and Shochet, 1986).

Identifying deficit groups or individuals to receive special attention invariably leads to problems of another kind. The provision of a separate learning service makes learning and study problems the responsibility of the specialist. It gives the message to teachers that they are not responsible for the learning strategies and skills of their students. It places the responsibility for student learning outside the teaching room, but still allows teachers and the institution to argue that they are doing something about the 'problem' of student learning. As a consequence of this deficit view of student learning, many students who would benefit from assistance from specialist study skills advisers are reluctant to approach them as they do not wish to be seen as having problems.

Integrated learning strategies programmes

Integrated learning strategies programmes combine the teaching of subject matter with the teaching of learning strategies relevant to the content or discipline of study. Integrated programmes include explicit teaching of learning strategies at the same time as teaching the subject matter, and also include guided practice in using the strategies. The learning strategies are not taught as additional content but are an integral part of the existing curricula and the learning goals of the subject. Derry and Murphy (1986) found that integrated programmes tend to include the following features:

- step-by-step procedures which provide directions on where, when and how to use the strategies
- 'think-aloud' modelling by the teacher or student
- supporting study questions and activities which require students to engage in targeted thinking processes
- study prompts and clues which provide reminders to use specific strategies

- information on the features of the strategies that make them useful and the range of learning situations in which they can be applied.

While there is no reason why these features cannot be incorporated into separate learning strategies programmes, they typically are not. Even if they were included, it would be unlikely that the separate programme would be as effective as an integrated programme with the same features because the strategies would not be embedded in the subject matter where their relevance and application could be clearly established.

Integrated programmes have been found to be more effective than separate learning strategies programmes in affecting the outcomes of student learning. For example, university students involved in integrated programmes developed by Cawley (1989) and Eizenberg (1988) were able to demonstrate analytical and critical thinking skills not often achieved by many university students (Dahlgren, 1984). Moreover, university students involved in our integrated programme demonstrated more effective learning than students taught in the conventional manner (Fuller et al., 1994).

Integrated programmes do not escape criticism. One criticism is that strategies learned in a particular context may not be used in other learning contexts. For example, strategies learnt in mathematics may not be transferred to language studies, even though they may be the most appropriate strategies to use. The danger with an integrated programme is that the strategies become so contextualized with the subject matter with which they were taught that students cannot separate the strategy from the context. This is less likely to occur if the features of the strategies that make them useful, and the range of learning situations in which they can be applied, are explicit parts of the teaching programme.

Should learning strategies be taught at university?
Regardless of the type of programme offered, the appropriateness of including learning strategies as part of a university curriculum has been challenged. Some university teachers argue that the majority of students do not need learning strategy assistance and that valuable teaching time is better spent on covering subject matter (Cloete and Shochet, 1986). This criticism often originates from an elitist view of university teaching which sees the inclusion of learning strategies as a concession to weaker or disadvantaged students who, it is felt, should not be attending university in the first place. However, it has been shown that students who benefit most from learning strategy instruction are the average and above average students, regardless of whether the programmes are taught in separate or integrated contexts (Cloete and Shochet, 1986).

Accordingly, if university learning is considered to be a developmental process, the role of teachers includes helping all students improve relative to their initial positions. The question then becomes not *if* learning strategies should be taught at university, but *how* they should be taught. While both separate and integrated learning strategies programmes have their relative strengths and weaknesses, the weight of evidence is that a well designed integrated programme will be more effective in teaching students learning strategies. This conclusion is supported by Candy *et al.* (1994) who argue strongly for all undergraduate courses to include learning strategies and skills as the central core of the curriculum, with the subject matter providing the context in which they are taught.

Controlling the use of learning strategies

Another important factor that influences the effectiveness of learning strategy programmes relates to who controls the use of the learning strategies. While learning strategies must always be carried out by the students, the selection and use of particular strategies may be controlled either by the teacher or by the student (Derry and Murphy, 1986).

The teacher may control the use of learning strategies in two ways. One way is for the teacher to set up a task so that a particular learning strategy must be used to complete it. The other way is for the teacher to explicitly require the student to use or demonstrate the particular strategy. In both of these situations the teacher makes the decision for the student. The teacher decides on the most appropriate strategies and sets up tasks and activities that require the students to use them. In such situations the students may not be aware of why they are using particular learning strategies or even that they are using them. Instructional design methodologies are an example of lesson-controlled strategies that promote cognitive processing without the student being aware of the strategies being used. They are similar to teacher-controlled programmes in which students are rarely made aware that they are using particular learning strategies (Gagné, 1985). Learning strategy programmes that are controlled by the teachers in this way are usually ineffective (Derry and Murphy, 1986). Students in these programmes do not seem to learn any more effectively than students who receive no learning strategy instruction.

The use of learning strategies is controlled by students when they select or decide on a particular strategy themselves. In some situations strategy selection and use may be deliberate, but in others it may be unconscious with a particular strategy being used because it is the only one known to the student. An example of deliberate strategy selection is when a student prepares for an exam by deciding to read the text, taking notes under a number of key headings, and memorizing the headings using a peg-word method. An example of unconscious strategy use is where a student who needs to remember several key points uses a mnemonic strategy because it is the only memory strategy known to the student.

Students' awareness or consciousness of the learning act is a crucial aspect of learning. The difference between successful and unsuccessful students is often not the teaching method or the specific strategy used, but whether the students were aware that they were using a specific learning strategy and why they were using it (Cloete and Shochet, 1986). Students who unconsciously select an appropriate learning strategy may learn effectively in that particular task. However, they are unlikely to learn other tasks effectively if the strategy is inappropriate. Students who unconsciously select strategies do not consider whether there might be more effective ways to learn the information.

Students need to be aware of the learning strategies they are using and the reasons why they are effective. Teachers need to consider ways in which they can provide instruction and practice in particular learning strategies, and also provide opportunities for students to control the use of the strategies.

Informing students about learning strategies

Teaching students about strategies and how to use them will not in itself cause them to use them when they should. Students often do not use strategies, even though the situation in which the strategies should be used is very similar to the situation in which they were learnt. Students are also unlikely to transfer strategies they have learned in one situation to a new situation even though they might be the most appropriate strategies for the task. The failure of students to maintain the use of learning strategies, or to transfer the use of learning strategies from one context to another, is a consistent finding of research on learning strategy instruction (Derry and Murphy, 1986; Pressley and McCormick, 1995). Unless the effectiveness of the new strategy compared to the old strategy is clearly established, students are unlikely to adopt the new one.

A number of studies have investigated why students do not continue to use learning strategies they have been taught. The usual design of these studies involved teaching one group of students a learning strategy for a task, and another group the same strategy and task but with the additional information of why, when and where the strategy could be used. These studies all drew the same conclusion: students who were informed about the usefulness of the strategy were more likely to use the strategy later than were students who did not receive the additional information (Pressley et al., 1984).

Clearly then, information that informs students on the usefulness of the strategy is an important component of a learning strategies programme. If the use of the strategy is to be maintained, students need to receive information on why, when and where the strategy can be used. But this is not all that is needed in a programme. While more students who receive the additional information use the strategy, a number of students in the informed group do not. Reasons for this are that students do not like using the particular strategy or do not think that the gains produced by the strategy are worth the effort (Rabinowitz *et al.*, 1992). Another reason is that students do not recognize the value of strategies to their learning.

Students are often unaware of how a strategy affects their learning. This is equally true for adults and children. Pressley and McCormick (1995) reviewed a number of studies where students were required to learn information using two strategies. One strategy was an effective strategy, the other an inefficient but commonly preferred strategy of most of the students. The efficient strategy produced the expected higher results. However, neither adults nor children were initially able to say which strategy was more effective. It took the results of the test to demonstrate the effectiveness of the strategy to them. Students who had the opportunity to compare the effectiveness of the two strategies continued to use the more effective strategy in later tasks.

Good learning strategy programmes include instruction not only on how to use a strategy but also why, when and where to use it. Teachers have commonly assumed that the value of a learning strategy will be clearly evident to students and that the provision of instruction and information is enough to convince them of its value. However, few programmes include explicit opportunities for students to compare the effects of one strategy with another. The usual way of teaching strategies and asking students to try them to see how they work is unlikely to convince many students that they should adopt the particular strategies (Pressley and McCormick, 1995). The opportunity for university students to compare the effectiveness of strategies can convince them of the usefulness of the strategy and provide them with a more meaningful understanding of its effectiveness (Nist *et al.*, 1991; Pressley and McCormick, 1995). University students need to be convinced that a strategy will improve their learning before they will put effort into becoming proficient in its use.

Most students have a preference for one or two strategies which they apply widely across a number of different tasks and subjects. If students can build up a large repertoire of effective learning strategies and know in what situations they are effective, they will be more able to tackle a wide range of tasks. Students with a flexible repertoire of strategies can generate alternative approaches that increase their chance of successfully solving a problem or completing a task (Weinstein *et al.*, 1989).

Increases in the effectiveness of education may come as much, or more, from helping students understand their own learning processes as varying your teaching. (Norman, 1976)

If students are to understand and gain control over their own learning, then teachers need to examine their current teaching methods and strategies and identify ways to teach students how to learn effectively.

A framework for teaching learning strategies

In spite of the interest of the research community in the teaching of learning strategies, there seems to be little evidence of changes in teaching practice and student learning.

Most teachers do not teach the many strategies that can improve academic perform-ance and learning, let alone do all that can be done to improve students' motivation to be cognitively active. (Pressley and McCormick, 1995, p. 10)

Identifying what, when and where to teach students learning strategies is now possible because of information provided by research findings of the learning strategy programmes. However, it seems that it is not yet clear how teachers should go about incorporating this information into their teaching practices.

Teachers at universities usually refer to teaching methods rather than teaching strategies. Teaching methods are commonly identified in terms of the situation in which teaching occurs: for example, lecture, tutorial, practical or laboratory methods. However, when the objective is to teach learning strategies in the context of the subject matter, then the actual teaching method becomes a less central issue. What does become central is the selection of teaching and learning strategies that will help students learn effectively.

An argument against the use of traditional university teaching methods was presented by Ramsden (1992). He suggested that the lecture-tutorial format used in most universities is detrimental to student learning. He identified a number of alternative methods and strategies from a variety of courses and disciplines that were demonstrably more effective. These teach-ing strategies provided greater opportunities for students to work with information, addressed student motivation and interest, established coopera-tive learning tasks, and involved students in decision-making. The teaching methods varied according to the teachers, subject discipline and organiza-tional constraints but they all actively involved students in acquiring know-ledge, interpreting results and testing hypotheses against reality in a cooperative learning context.

Essential aspects of teaching learning strategies

University teachers should encourage students to adopt a deep approach to their learning (Gibbs, 1992; Ramsden, 1992). This becomes even more impor-tant when learning strategies are taught in an integrated programme. Unless students adopt a deep approach to learning, they will not practise learning strategies that develop understanding, but will continue to use less effective strategies (Ramsden et al., 1986).

Biggs and Telfer (1987) and Gibbs (1992) suggest that university teachers should address four aspects in order to encourage students to adopt a deep approach: intrinsic motivation, active involvement in learning, interaction with others, and development of a well-structured knowledge base. If teachers do not address these aspects, then it is unlikely that attempts to teach learning strategies will be successful.

Motivational aspects of student learning can be addressed by establishing a positive emotional climate in the learning situation. This is not easy to achieve, and requires commitment on the part of both teachers and students. Establishing a positive emotional climate requires that teachers communicate their aims and expectations to students. Teachers also need to listen to students and address their legitimate needs and concerns. Effective two-way communication ensures that teachers and students are clear on what each is trying to achieve. There is a great deal of evidence to show that positive emotional and motivational learning climates are more likely to lead to intrinsic learning for understanding. On the other hand, when there is a high level of anxiety and an emphasis on assessment then students are more likely to learn to reproduce knowledge for extrinsic reasons (Ames, 1992; Biggs and Telfer, 1987; Gibbs, 1992).

Students need to be *active participants* in the learning process rather than passive recipients of information. This means that the teacher must plan learning tasks so that students have the opportunity to work with information actively in order to process it, relate it to their existing knowledge and the wider topic or course of study, and reflect upon it. This can be facilitated by developing activities that require students to acquire information, work with information and confirm learning. The task-focused learning strategies in Part Two of this book provide a number of learning tasks that require students to be actively involved in their learning.

The purpose of *interacting with others* is to provide students with opportunities to manipulate ideas and negotiate meaning. This is best done in supportive groups in which the learning climate is positive. Interaction can take many forms. Tutorials and seminars are the more usual forums for student-teacher and student-student interaction, but autonomous student groups and peer tutoring are two other forms that can promote more effective learning (Gibbs, 1992). These can be formally established and facilitated by the teacher. For example, the teacher can organize meeting rooms, provide guidelines for tutorless tutorials, establish the organization of the groups, and set group tasks and assessments. Informal groups can be facilitated by teachers encouraging students to set up informal study groups. Many students come to university with the belief that working with other students is a form of cheating. Encouraging them to work with other students and suggesting ways in which they can study together are often all that is required for students to establish their own groups. If teachers also inform students of times they can be contacted to answer questions that arise from these study groups, it sends the students a clear message that interaction is supported and valued. The teaching and learning strategies in Part Two include many suggestions and activities aimed at promoting student interaction.

Students need a *well-structured knowledge base* in order to think and learn. It is impossible to understand, to think critically, or to analyse and solve problems without first acquiring a sound knowledge base.

The earlier section on the information processing approach to learning established the importance of relating new information to what was already known, and of structuring and organizing the new information so that it is encoded and stored to facilitate further learning. Because of the way in which cognitive processes work, it is vital that prior knowledge be activated so that students can make sense of new information and concepts. To facilitate effective learning, the teacher should help students relate new knowledge to other knowledge rather than introducing it in isolation. The information needs to be well-structured, clearly presented and taught as an integrated whole rather than as isolated pieces. The strategies outlined previously for acquiring information, and detailed in Part Two, are directed at helping students' learning to be structured, organized and linked to previous knowledge.

These aspects of motivation, active involvement in the learning task, interaction with others and a well-structured knowledge base are essential in any programme designed to teach learning strategies. With these aspects established as the basis of any teaching programme, a number of teaching strategies can be used to further promote student learning.

Strategies for teaching

Gibbs (1992) described a number of teaching strategies which promote effective student learning. Many of these overlap and should be seen as complementary rather than alternative strategies. A brief outline of these strategies follows.

The *fine tuning strategy* involves the modification of conventional practices or existing structures in order to increase motivation, learner activity and interaction, and to utilize a well-structured knowledge base. Changes in methods may take place in:

- lectures, by introducing active learning tasks and peer-group discussions in typically passive lecture classes. Buzz pairs where students discuss their response to a question with the person next to them is an effective strategy for involving students in the lecture situation
- reading, through the use of reading guides or the division of background reading between members of small teams, followed by peer tutoring. This is called a jigsaw strategy and is described more fully in Part Two. Self-directed learning materials are another effective way to guide students' reading and to provide a background for group discussion (Chalmers, 1995)

- seminars or tutorials, through the use of tutorless tutorial groups, student-led discussions, and group work. Self-directed study materials can also guide student work in group work and tutorless tutorials
- laboratory work, by replacing selected tutor-designed laboratory tasks with student-designed laboratory tasks and with peer review of the work
- field work, by introducing independent student-designed fieldwork within a given framework.

The *independent learning strategy* involves giving students more autonomy and control over the subject matter, learning methods, pace of study and the formal assessment of learning. Teaching methods include the use of learning contracts, self- and peer assessment, project work, and self-directed learning materials. It may also involve negotiation with students on goals, learning methods, assignments, assessment methods, assessment criteria and marks.

The *personal development strategy* emphasizes motivational aspects of learning, especially students' personal involvement in learning. The role of the teacher is to create a safe and supportive learning climate, to facilitate student responsibility and autonomy, and to emphasize expression of feelings and sensitive response to others. Teaching methods include group work, discussion, and various other methods that allow for students' expression of feelings and covering the course content.

The *problem-based strategy* involves learning through tackling relevant problems. The aim is to learn rather than to solve the problems. The main features are the identification of relevant problems, a desire or 'need to know', the integration of knowledge from a number of sources, and interaction and cooperation. The opportunity for reflection on both content and processes of learning helps students take charge of their learning, even in highly constrained circumstances. This method is particularly relevant where the aim is to turn experience into learning. Teaching methods include the use of learning diaries, reflective journals and portfolios of work, discussions of learning strategies, reflective exercises, and the use of video, audio and observers to provide feedback on performance or skills.

The *independent group work strategy* focuses on interaction between students. Teaching methods include group-based project work and peer tutoring. It can include other strategies such as problem-based learning or conventional in-class activities such as student-led seminar groups.

The *learning-by-doing strategy* utilizes experiential learning and emphasizes learner activity. The focus is on the deliberate introduction of concrete experience of real-world tasks to encourage students to become more involved, more active, and more aware of their existing knowledge-base and its use in their concrete experience. Teaching methods include the use of games, simulations, role plays, visits, and practical work and work experience.

The purpose of *project work* is to go beyond the reproduction of information to the application of knowledge. Project work requires a sound knowledge base if it is to be used successfully. It can be a highly motivating strategy, particularly when students are involved in the development or selection of the project. It is a strategy that results in a high level of student activity and involvement.

Gibbs (1992) emphasized that simply using these teaching strategies will not necessarily result in students learning more effectively. Group or independent work strategies can be used to achieve trivial or superficial learning outcomes. Project work can involve a great deal of purposeless busy-work. It is important that teachers implement teaching strategies with the intention of fostering students' deep understanding of the subject matter and their learning processes. If strategies are implemented with this intention and are embedded in a programme that incorporates the four key aspects of motivation, active learner involvement, interaction with others, and a well-structured knowledge base, then students are more likely to learn effectively and achieve a deep understanding of the subject matter (Gibbs, 1992).

The use of teaching strategies such as these, and a learning strategies programme where learning strategies are explicitly taught in the context of regular course work, will encourage students to adopt a deep approach to their learning and provide them with the cognitive tools needed to learn.

Teaching learning strategies is not easy

At this time it is appropriate to reflect on what is involved in teaching learning strategies to university students and what can be achieved by doing this. Teaching learning strategies is not as straightforward as might have been implied up to now. It is not easy to change students' approaches to learning and achieve positive learning outcomes (Fuller *et al.*, 1994; Gibbs, 1992). Students do not readily change from a surface approach to a deep approach, and if such change occurs, it can be quite temporary.

Students' preferred approaches to learning

The most common approach to learning used by students at university is the surface approach (Gibbs, 1992). Gibbs observed that it was not only poor students who demonstrated surface approaches, nor were surface approaches only found in poor university courses. The surface approach was the dominant approach of all students across a wide range of courses, and was still the dominant approach even after innovative programmes designed to foster deep learning had been implemented. Moreover, the students who participated in our learning strategies programmes over one semester (Chalmers *et al.*, 1992) and a subsequent programme over one year (Fuller *et al.*,

1993) used the same approaches to learning as students who had not partici- pated in the programmes. While Biggs (1987) argued that the surface ap- proach is a pathological response to schooling, its pervasiveness and resistance to change suggests that it should be viewed as adaptive rather than pathological. There are many instances cited in the psychological literature where strategies are adopted in order to reduce effort (eg, Salomon and Globerson, 1987; Scardamalia and Bereiter, 1986). Effort-reducing strategies have been identified in a variety of tasks: for example, the copy-delete note-taking strategy (Brown and Day, 1983), the knowledge-telling writing strategy (Scardamalia and Bereiter, 1986), and the single-step planning strat- egy (Chalmers and Lawrence, 1993). Similarly, the surface approach to learn- ing can be viewed as an effort-reducing strategy. In common with other effort-reducing strategies, the surface approach results in the completion of the task in a way that ensures that the demands of the task are just met or 'satisficed' (Biggs, 1993a). Viewing the surface strategy as an adaptive strategy explains why it is so common. However, just as the effort-reducing strategies result in barely adequate outcomes, so too is effective learning rarely achieved by students who adopt a surface approach. It is important that the use of the surface approach by students is not rewarded or encouraged either by teaching or assessment practices.

Different students approach their learning in different ways irrespective of the course or subject matter. In many of the programmes reviewed, students who adopted a surface approach to learning worked alongside students who adopted a deep approach (Gibbs, 1992). However, it was also found that some students changed their approach when they worked in a group. Students who regularly worked in groups adopted the dominant learning approach of the group, even when it was different from their preferred approach. Working in groups does not automatically ensure that students adopt a deep approach to learning, but it does create a situation in which it is possible to instigate a change in students' approaches to learning.

Not only will there be variations in students' approaches to learning within a given group of students, but students may vary their approaches to learning during a course of study and across courses of study. They may move from a surface approach at the beginning of their university study to a deep approach by the end of their course or, as has been found to be more common, from a deep approach at the beginning of university to a surface approach at the end of university study (Gibbs, 1992; Volet and Chalmers, 1992). The expectation that students will naturally progress from a surface approach to a deep approach as they move through university is not supported by the research (eg, Biggs, 1987; Gibbs, 1992; Ramsden, 1992). More students adopt a surface approach as they progress through university, particularly in courses where there is little focus on higher level cognitive learning outcomes.

This variety and variability in students' approaches to learning should be viewed positively. It means that it is possible to change the ways in which students approach their learning. The structure, content, and way the groups are structured and organized can lead to changes in the ways in which students approach their learning.

Changing students' approaches to learning through teaching learning strategies

Learning strategy programmes introduced in university courses have produced mixed results. Some lecturers report success in terms of positive effects on students' approaches to learning (Gibbs, 1992) and the outcomes of their learning (Fuller *et al.*, 1994). Other programmes have resulted in few gains in terms of grades or study inventory measures when comparisons are made with students who did not participate in the learning strategy programme. However, the findings also show that the students involved in the learning strategies programmes responded positively about the personal gains they felt they had made (Gibbs, 1992; Ramsden, 1992). It is often difficult to measure the effects of learning programmes, but it is more positive and more appropriate to view learning strategy programmes as being at least as effective as conventional programmes, with the possibility of greater gains over the longer term.

Programmes that are implemented in the early years of a course of study, and are followed up by continued learning support, have a greater effect on the way in which students go about their learning. Gibbs (1992) found that students in their first year were more responsive to learning strategies programmes, and more likely to adopt a deep approach to their learning, than third-year students who adopted few of the learning strategies and rarely changed their approaches to learning.

It is important to caution that the effects of programmes have generally been found to be short lived and restricted to the immediate course of study in which the programme was implemented (Gibbs, 1992; Fuller *et al.*, 1994). Students who participated in our programme, and students in programmes reviewed by Gibbs, quickly reverted to their previous lower level patterns when they returned to conventional courses of study. It would seem that the approach adopted by students relies heavily on the context of learning. While it is encouraging to know that change is possible when setting up a programme, it is also important to keep in mind that improving only one course in a programme of study is unlikely to have a lasting impact on students. It requires a consistent and coordinated approach to produce permanent changes in students' approaches to learning.

One of the most effective ways to influence students' learning is through assessment practices. Learning programmes that were not accompanied by changes in the assessment practices had minimal effect on student learning approaches. Important messages from the review of learning programmes and from studies on the impact of assessment are that assessment practices should reward students who adopt a deep approach to their learning, and that the requirements and criteria on which assessments are marked should be made clear to students.

Variations in teaching methods do not appear to have much effect on student learning. Learning strategy programmes that use lecture-tutorial methods are as effective as alternative methods. The actual subject matter also has little effect on student learning. What is important is the design of the learning strategies programmes. The learning processes and tasks that engage the students are more important than the teaching methods used or the subject matter selected (Gibbs, 1992; Ramsden, 1992). Learning experiences should focus on promoting the active learning of students rather than on the delivery of subject matter. The role of the teacher in effective learning strategy programmes is to organize appropriate learning opportunities and to provide support to the development of students' independent learning.

Changing the ways teachers teach and the ways classes are conducted is never easy. Therefore, the process of implementing change should be seen as evolutionary rather than revolutionary. All the learning strategies programmes discussed were developed and modified over a number of semesters and, in some cases, over a number of years. Many of the programmes resulted in few changes in student learning in their first semester of implementation (Gibbs, 1992). It takes time and experience with a new programme to identify problems and make appropriate adjustments. It also takes time to develop and fine tune the teaching skills required to implement a programme. These teaching skills are unlikely to involve lecturing and presentation skills but, rather, skills such as explaining, devising student activities, modelling thinking and reasoning processes, designing assessments that require higher levels of cognitive processing, identifying appropriate criteria in assessments, and asking questions that lead to reflection and deeper processing. Skills such as these take time, practice and considerable fine tuning to refine.

One way in which to maintain the momentum and to build skills is to establish a group of supportive colleagues. Programmes developed and implemented by teams have been more successful than programmes developed by individuals working in isolation (Chalmers *et al.*, 1994; Gibbs, 1992; Ramsden, 1992).

Individuals working on their own can feel isolated and suffer from lack of feedback and support for their work and ideas. Support does not have to be provided from within the teachers' own group or department, though it is highly beneficial when it is. Support can be provided by others who are involved in developing programmes in other departments or courses, or by colleagues and friends who are prepared to attend classes to provide support and constructive feedback. In Part Three of this book a number of university teachers emphasize the importance of supportive colleagues when developing a learning strategies programme.

The role of students in providing feedback and support to teachers should not be underestimated. Students can be discriminating consumers of educational practices. Soliciting student support and responses to the various approaches and activities used in a programme can be a valuable source of information on the effectiveness of the programme. Students can provide information on their own learning processes and progress, and on their impressions of the teaching methods and processes. However, information from students should be treated thoughtfully for it may be based on students' preference for tasks that require a surface approach.

There is much to be gained from developing a programme designed to enhance student learning. Gains can result for students in terms of their approach to learning, their depth of cognitive processing and their ability to control and direct their learning. Gains can also result for teachers in terms of achieving their goals of university education, and enabling their students to learn more effectively in their subject discipline by developing and extending their own teaching skills and practices.

Chapter 4:

The Effect of Assessment on Learning

Student learning is affected by a number of factors, including the quality of teaching, student approaches to learning, and access to and availability of appropriate resources. However, the most powerful single influence on the quality of student learning is probably the assessment system that is used (Crooks, 1988; Gibbs, 1992). Assessment systems may encourage students to use strategies that will help them learn the subject matter effectively or lead them to use less effective strategies. Students will typically use strategies that reward them in terms of marks or grades. For example, assessment methods that allow students to obtain high marks by simply reproducing material they have learned encourage students to adopt a surface approach to their learning (Biggs and Telfer, 1987; Gibbs, 1992). Therefore, to encourage students to adopt a deep approach to their learning and to use appropriate learning strategies it is important to ensure that the assessment system supports the type of learning promoted by the teacher and the university.

It is important to differentiate between the two major functions of assessment. One function of assessment is to enable the university to grade students and to certify that they have met course requirements. This involves using formal assessment tasks such as tests, examinations, assignments and projects. Typically the main emphasis is on finding out how much students have learned and making a summative judgement about the adequacy of their performance. A second and quite different function of assessment is to support student learning. This usually involves using less formal assessment tasks aimed at finding out about the quality of students' learning, providing students with feedback, and suggesting ways in which they can improve their learning and understanding.

These distinct and often conflicting functions of assessment have implications for the ways in which students approach and carry out their learning. For example, when students are being assessed in order to support their learning, it does not matter if they demonstrate some lack of understanding or skill, for this provides the teachers and students with an indication of an aspect of learning that needs attention. In assessment situations such as these, students can be encouraged to tackle difficult tasks without being threatened by the prospect of failure. On the other hand, if students are being assessed for grading purposes, any demonstrated lack of understanding has important implications for the grade they receive. In grading situations it is important for students to conceal a lack of understanding and limitations in their learning in whatever way they can in order to gain enough marks to achieve their goals.

Many university teachers place emphasis on the grading function of assessment and overlook its function in supporting learning. This distorts the learning process, as illustrated by the following comment from a student:

There's an awful lot of work being done up here for the wrong reasons . . . people are going through here and not learning anything at all. . . . There are a lot of courses where you can learn what's necessary to get the grade and when you come out of the class you don't know anything at all. You haven't learned a damn thing really. In fact, if you try to really learn something, it would handicap you as far as getting a grade goes. (Becker *et al.*, cited in Ramsden, 1992, p.68)

In a review of research on the impact of assessment on student learning, Crooks (1988) drew attention to some effects that assessment can have on how students go about their learning. Some of the more important effects are summarized below.

Student expectations of what will be assessed

Students often report that the way they are assessed in their university courses affects what they intend to learn and how they go about their learning. The following comment from a second-year student of psychology illustrates this:

In the class test, if you can give a bit of factual information, so-and-so did that, and concluded that, for two sides of writing, then you'll get a good mark. I hate to say it, but what you've got to do is have a list of the 'facts'. You write down ten important points and memorize those – then you'll do all right in the class test. (Ramsden, 1992, p.70)

Such expectations of what will be assessed have a powerful influence on the approach to learning adopted by students. For example, if students expect examination questions that simply require them to reproduce learned material and not demonstrate that they understand it, they are likely to use a surface approach when studying for the examination. This will lead to only a limited understanding of the subject matter. If the papers are marked in a way that accepts or rewards the reproduction of memorized material, the students will be able to obtain high marks and will not be discouraged from using surface approaches in the future. On the other hand, if it is made clear that they have to show that they understand the subject matter, they are more likely to use strategies that will help them achieve a deeper understanding of that subject matter.

The implications for university teachers are clear. They should explicitly inform students of the level of learning that is required to obtain a pass grade. It should be made clear that students will be required to do more than just reproduce subject matter, and will be expected to work with the material in a cognitively demanding way. The teacher must ensure that assessment tasks are cognitively demanding. This will encourage students to adopt a deeper approach to their learning.

Frequency of assessment

Assessment can have positive effects on student learning. For example, when a test is imminent, students are likely to devote more time to studying the subject matter. After the test, if students receive feedback about the quality of their performance, they may use the information to guide their study in the future. However, this does not mean that more assessment will result in better learning. The potential benefits of assessment can be lost if students are assessed too often. Frequent assessment makes it hard for students to allocate time to prepare properly for a test or to study a topic thoughtfully in order to develop a good understanding of it. This difficulty is compounded when students study a number of courses which are over-assessed. Assessment that is frequently administered will tend to be superficial and require only the reproduction of information, because it is difficult to get students to manage a number of challenging tasks over a short period of time. In brief, assessment that is too frequent leads students to adopt surface approaches to learning.

Accordingly, university teachers should avoid over-assessment, especially for the purpose of assigning grades. On the other hand they should provide frequent opportunities for students to monitor their progress and receive feedback on the quality of their learning in informal and non-threatening situations.

Standards used to grade student work

Another aspect of the assessment system that affects the quality of learning is the standard of work students are expected to achieve. In general, the research indicates that conveying high expectations to students is reflected in higher achievement, providing the expectations are realistic. However, if expectations are perceived to be unrealistic, many students, especially those who have not achieved well previously, will not attempt to meet them (Crooks, 1988; Pressley and McCormick, 1995).

It is helpful to students if they are given a clear idea of the standards of work that are expected of them. University teachers can help students develop an understanding of these standards by providing them with detailed criteria prior to beginning the task, and by giving them feedback on their performance and indicating what they could have done to improve their performance.

Many universities use a norm-referenced grading system which defines standards in terms of the number of students who can obtain the various grades, and which limits the number of students who can achieve high grades. This type of grading does not give students any information about what they should do in order to achieve at a high level. Most students are aware of where they stand in comparison to others taking the same course, and know that they can get a higher grade only if someone else receives a lower grade. Unless they think they have a reasonable chance of improving enough to perform better that the usual high achievers, there is little incentive for them to try to improve their grades.

Norm-referenced grading has been found to increase students' anxiety and reduce their sense of being responsible for the quality of their learning. It also reduces intrinsic motivation, limits the effectiveness of teacher feedback, and reduces the level of cooperation that occurs between students (Biggs and Moore, 1993; Crooks, 1988; Pressley and McCormick, 1995). It is better to grade on the basis of the quality of learning rather than the order of merit. This can be done by specifying in advance the specific qualitative criteria that will be used to grade students' work.

Type of assessment

University teachers are able to select from a wide range of assessments such as essay tests, objective tests, projects, practical examinations and critical reviews. Some of these types of assessment are more challenging to students than others. The type of assessment used can affect the way that students approach their learning. At first glance the research does not support this statement. For example, there has been little difference observed between the study behaviour of students expecting to be assessed with an essay test and that of students expecting an objective test (Crooks, 1988). However, closer examination of the results shows that this is true only when the students expect the level of the questions to test a particular level of understanding. If students expect to have to reproduce learned material, it does not seem to matter whether they are tested with an essay or an objective test. The level of understanding that is required affects the type of learning far more than the type of assessment (Clift and Imrie, 1981).

However, many students have clear beliefs about the cognitive demands associated with different assessment tasks. For example, most students would expect a critical review to be more demanding than a descriptive essay, and so would be likely to study differently for these two tasks.

Therefore, university teachers should be cautious about using types of assessment that might be perceived by students as requiring only a surface approach, such as short answer and multiple choice tests and descriptive essays. When using these types of assessment, teachers should stress that they will expect high levels of cognitive processing, and should give students some sample items to illustrate this.

Apart from the above caution, university teachers should select assessment tasks according to what is appropriate to the teaching and learning context, and use a mix of different tasks in order to give students the best opportunity to demonstrate the quality of their learning.

Some guidelines for assessment

It is clear that assessment affects students in many ways. It guides their decisions about what is important to learn, affects their motivation and perceptions of self-competence, influences their approaches to learning, directs their timing of personal study, consolidates learning and affects the extent to which enduring learning strategies and skills develop. The most vital message that has emerged from research is that teachers should give appropriate emphasis in their assessments to the strategies, skills, knowledge and attitudes that they believe are the most important. Some of these important learning outcomes may be hard to evaluate, but it is important that teachers find ways to do so, and not be satisfied with what is easy to assess. The challenge for university teachers is to assess in a way that affects students positively, so that the assessment process supports their efforts to promote quality learning. Many strategies, skills and attitudes we want our students to acquire can take years to develop. Their development can be undermined by inconsistent and inappropriate assessment practices.

In the context of teaching students to use appropriate learning strategies, it is especially important to use assessment practices that encourage students to adopt a deep approach to their learning. The following guidelines are intended to help university teachers do this. Some of the guidelines contradict conventional advice about assessment, much of which is intended to increase the accuracy of grades. For example, the suggestion that teachers should be prepared to sacrifice some reliability in favour of quality and authenticity may not be acceptable to a university administrator who sees assessment solely in terms of its grading function. Likewise university teachers who hold a quantitative conception of teaching, and see it as the process of transmitting information from an informed teacher to an uninformed student, will probably be uncomfortable with the suggestion that students should participate in developing the assessment package.

Focus on assessments that support learning

Too much emphasis is usually placed on the grading function of assessment, and too little on its role in helping students to learn. University teachers cannot avoid assessing for grading, but they should ensure that their assessment is not dominated by the grading function. They should try to make each formal assessment task a significant learning experience for students. Teachers should also help students learn to manage these tasks. In the section on strategies for confirming learning in Part Two of this book, information is provided on how teachers can do this.

There are also many informal assessment activities that can be used in class to support student learning. A comprehensive guide to these activities is provided by Angelo and Cross (1993).

Focus on assessing understanding

Assessment practices should emphasize understanding, the transfer of learning to untaught problems or situations, and critical and analytical thinking skills. The evaluation of knowledge of subject matter and the use of strategies and skills should take place through tasks that involve more than recognition or recall. It is better to set challenging tasks that require students to work with the subject matter, and not just reproduce it. However, it is insufficient just to *set* challenging tasks: these tasks must be *marked* in a way that focuses on understanding, and students should be given feedback about the quality of understanding shown in their work.

One problem associated with assessing for understanding is that it becomes more difficult to assign marks reliably to student work. Since students construct their own understanding of subject matter, teachers cannot expect that all students will respond to the task in the same way. Some university teachers address this problem by setting lower level tasks, or by using assessment formats (eg, multiple choice tests) that are easier to mark reliably. However, such a response will be counterproductive in the long term if it encourages students to adopt a surface approach to their learning. In terms of student learning it is better to sacrifice some reliability of assessment in favour of overall quality and authenticity.

Provide informative feedback to students

Assessment to support learning should aim to provide students with feedback. Feedback is most effective if it focuses students' attention on their progress in mastering important learning tasks. Feedback should be provided while it is still relevant, that is, as soon as possible after the task is completed. Feedback is most effective when students have the opportunity to improve their learning by resubmitting their work in response to the feedback. Finally, feedback should be quite specific and related to students' needs. Criticism that simply identifies deficiencies is rarely productive. Strategies for providing informative feedback to students are presented in Part Two of this book.

Encourage cooperation between students

Research studies consistently show that cooperation between students can enhance learning (eg, Pressley and McCormick, 1995; Slavin, 1983). Assessment tasks that facilitate cooperation between students (eg, projects conducted by small groups) are particularly effective in promoting student learning and motivation, and in developing interpersonal skills and relationships. They are especially appropriate for more complex tasks in which the different perspectives and skills of group members can complement each other.

Particular challenges arise when cooperative assessment tasks are used to contribute to students' grades. A question that arises is: should all students who participate in a cooperative assessment task receive the same grade, or should each receive a grade in proportion to his or her contribution? It is beyond the scope of this section to consider this matter in detail: guidelines for handling it are provided by Conway *et al.* (1993) and Goldfinch and Raeside (1990).

Set and clarify standards

Students learn best when standards are high and attainable. Assessment requirements and criteria should be made clear before an important task is attempted so that students can avoid misdirected effort. One way of clarifying standards is to involve students in working out the marking key that will be used to assess their work. This gives them an opportunity to find out how much importance will be placed on such matters as critical thinking, use of literature and the amount of subject matter presented.

Allow students to participate in the assessment process

Students are more likely to respond positively to assessment tasks if they have been involved in setting those tasks (Gibbs, 1992). There are many ways of getting students to participate in assessment decisions. For example, teachers can get students to help specify the requirements for a major assignment or project, and to suggest individual variations of an existing topic. Students can be allowed to decide for themselves how they will be assessed, such as by projects, essays, workshop activities or examinations. Students can participate directly in the assessment process by using self- and peer assessment activities. Activities of this type can make a significant contribution to enhancing intrinsic motivation.

Conclusion

Students have clear views on how to pass their courses, and what they have to do in order to get good marks. Student views are not always correct and they may differ from teachers' views, but they dominate the ways in which students go about learning (Gibbs, 1992). Programmes that teach learning strategies but do not include changes to the way in which the learning is assessed have little effect on the quality of student learning. It is only when assessment methods require students to demonstrate a deep understanding, and when the demands of the assessment are made explicit, that students change their perceptions of what they have to do, make appropriate changes to their study approach, and achieve a significant change in the quality of their learning. 'If only one change is to be made to a course or unit, then it should be the way in which assessment is carried out' (Gibbs, 1992, p.18).

Chapter 5:

Review of Learning and Teaching at University

Drawing on the previous chapters outlining the principles of good teaching and student learning, it is worth highlighting the following points. These should guide university teachers' thinking when they develop a learning strategies programme.

Beliefs about learning affect approaches to learning

The way in which students view their learning affects the way they approach their learning. Students do not always engage fully in the learning process and may take short cuts in order to meet course requirements with a minimum of effort. Students need encouragement to work with information at a high level if they are to understand it and achieve the goals of university learning.

Beliefs about teaching affect approaches to teaching

The way in which teachers view teaching affects the way they approach their teaching. Teachers who view teaching as the transmission of information from the teacher to the student often unwittingly encourage students to adopt a surface approach to learning. Teachers who view teaching as a process of facilitating learning are more likely to encourage students to learn with understanding and monitor the quality of their learning.

Both teachers and students are responsible for learning

Both the teacher and the student have a role to play in the teaching and learning of subject matter. However, teachers have a special responsibility to facilitate student learning. They can do this by explicitly teaching learning strategies and modelling their use. They should also provide opportunities for students to apply the strategies and give students feedback about how well they use them.

Students bring valuable learning experiences to the learning context

Students bring a wealth of knowledge, experience and skills to university. They may not be able to apply this immediately in the university learning context, but this does not diminish its value. Teachers who can identify and use their students' existing knowledge and skills are likely to increase their motivation, application of knowledge and understanding.

Learning strategies can be taught and learned

Learning strategies are not something that students have or do not have. Learning strategies can be taught and learned. The extent to which they are learned and applied flexibly by students depends on:

- whether students know a wide range of learning strategies
- how aware students are of when, where and why the strategy can be used
- the extent to which students have practised using strategies in a number of different contexts
- whether students have had the opportunity to compare the effectiveness of a new strategy with their preferred strategy.

Learning takes place best in a relevant context

Learning strategies should be taught in the context of a subject discipline. Integrated learning programmes are more effective in developing learning strategies, as both the subject matter and the strategies for learning it are taught together. The extent to which students transfer their use of learning strategies to a different context depends on how aware they are of the strategies being used.

The learning environment affects student learning

Teachers need to ensure that the learning environment encourages learning. They should consider ways to motivate their students, actively involve them in the learning process, increase opportunities for them to interact and work with each other, and help them build a well-structured knowledge base. These four aspects should form the basis of any learning strategies programme.

It is not easy to change

It is difficult for both teachers and students to change familiar practices and it is easy to revert to what is comfortable and has worked in the past, particularly when under pressure to meet deadlines or when facing difficulties. Teachers and students both have to leave their comfort zone when they embark on a learning strategies programme. In particular, teachers cannot expect to challenge their students when they have not first challenged themselves.

Assessment affects learning

Students will adopt an approach to learning that enables them to meet the assignment requirements of the course. Therefore, the assessment practices should reflect the objectives of the programme and course. The objectives and criteria for assessment should be clearly articulated by the teachers. Assessment should focus on the desired student outcomes, not on repetition and the retention of isolated pieces of information.

These points provide the underlying framework of the learning and teaching strategies described in Part Two.

Part 2: Learning and teaching strategies

Chapter 6:

Introduction

In Part Two we present a number of learning strategies that we have taught to our students. First we explain the importance of each strategy and describe what it involves. Then we describe one method of teaching it that we have found to be effective. Finally, we describe some class activities that allow students to practise using the strategy while they are learning the subject matter of the course.

We have organized the strategies under the task-focused headings described in Part One. *Strategies for acquiring information* are primarily concerned with collecting and organizing subject matter that has to be learned. *Strategies for working with information* focus on activities that students can use to develop their understanding of the subject matter, while *strategies for confirming learning* are used when students are preparing to meet the assessment requirements of a course of study. *Personal management strategies* are directed at students' management of their personal study.

To some extent these subdivisions may be misleading, since we get students to use all the strategies in a way that enhances their understanding of the subject matter. Therefore all strategies could probably have been presented under the heading 'Strategies for working with information'. However, we find it convenient to classify them according to their primary purpose. For example, the strategy 'Note making from text' is included in the section 'Strategies for acquiring information' because it is most commonly used when students are reading to acquire relevant information. However, we recognize that when students use the recommended method to make notes from their readings they also develop their understanding of the subject matter.

In describing how to teach these strategies, we have chosen to present the process in a series of numbered steps. You may not feel that it is necessary to follow all the steps that we have suggested. Although we encourage you to adapt the suggested procedures to meet your particular circumstances, we advise you to be cautious when you do this. The steps we use to teach the strategies are based on well-established principles of learning described in Part One. Any changes you make should be informed by these principles. Colleagues who have taught these strategies have told us that they found all the steps were necessary, even when they thought that their students would not need to follow them. They reported that their students generally knew less about learning strategies than they had expected, and that omitting a step reduced the effectiveness of strategy instruction. This required them to go back and re-teach the strategy.

We have indicated the approximate time that is needed to teach each strategy. You might think that we have overestimated the time required for some of them. However, we have found that teaching these strategies often takes more time than expected, and that the quality of instruction suffers if sufficient time is not available to follow all the recommended steps. Therefore we suggest that you do not attempt to teach a strategy unless you have available the time that we have indicated is necessary for that strategy.

In writing this part of the book we have assumed that readers will be familiar with the teaching strategies that are commonly used in universities. It is beyond the scope of the book to present details of these teaching strategies, which are covered in texts such as Barry and King (1993), Brown and Atkins (1988), Gibbs and Habeshaw (1988), and Newble and Cannon (1989). However, we have included a brief section on teaching strategies in order to draw your attention to some matters that are particularly important when teaching learning strategies in the way that we recommend. For example, since we place considerable importance on cooperative learning, we thought it necessary to give some advice on teaching small groups. When you introduce an innovation it is important to clarify expectations with students, so we have outlined ways of doing this.

Our research and teaching experience have taught us that effective strategy instruction requires careful preparation and planning. You must ensure that you understand the particular strategy you intend to teach, and are skilful in its use. You should be able to explain why the strategy is effective, by relating it to relevant principles of learning. Then, if students suggest changes to the way the strategy is used, you will be able to help them determine what effect these changes would have on the quality of learning. Finally, you should be enthusiastic and confident when teaching the strategies and explaining their benefits to students. They work.

Chapter 7:

Strategies for Acquiring Information

The strategies presented in this chapter are used to identify and organize information that students have to learn. This is an important and necessary process if students are to learn with understanding. Although it is possible to acquire information first and then try to understand it later, it is better to link the two processes together so that students develop an understanding of the information as they acquire it.

The methods that we use for teaching these strategies integrate the processes of acquisition and understanding. When students follow our recommended method for making notes, they will also develop a better understanding of the content of the lecture or reading. When they skim read to find information quickly, they will also get an understanding of what the reading is about.

- Accessing information
- Identifying main points from lectures and readings
- Memorizing information
- Note making for assignments
- Note making from lectures: following the lecturer's structure
- Note making from lectures: using a structure developed from prior reading
- Note making from text
- Skim reading

Accessing information

Introduction

Modern information systems make it easy for students to obtain up-to-date information. However, many students are not skilled at using these systems, and some deliberately avoid using them. Unless they become skilful in using these systems, they will have to work with outdated information and will not be able to access new information effectively.

Description

The skills involved in accessing information include using the following:

- on-line library catalogues
- CD ROM or on-line information indexes
- Various media such as print, audio, video, or microfiche
- the 'Virtual Campus' and Internet
- the World Wide Web.

Teaching students to access information

Time required: two sessions of about 20 minutes

Most university libraries or information systems have staff available to help students learn how to access information by using on-line catalogue or computer databases. You should collaborate with them in teaching students how to access information. They have special expertise with the systems, while you are expert in the subject matter that students are working on in class.

If you want to teach them to search a library catalogue or an on-line database you might engage in the following activities:

1. Select an important question related to subject matter you are teaching.
2. Consult with the library staff and plan a search around key terms connected with that question.
3. In class, present the question to the students and assign them a specific task associated with it. For example, you might ask them to use a particular database to find readings that relate to the question and then summarize one of the articles they locate. Tell students that the information they collect will be used as the basis for activities in the next class session.
4. Get the library staff to conduct a session with students in which they search the database for relevant information. Since you have identified key terms with the librarians, they will be able to work with the students in an informed and focused way.

---

5. In the next class use the information that students have found to address the original question.
6. Have students review and discuss the search processes that were used.

Using this strategy in class activities

There are a number of activities you can use to develop and maintain skill at accessing information. For example:

- Present a question associated with subject matter that you are teaching and get students to use a particular database to find recent evidence relating to that question. Ask each student to produce a print-out of the results of the search and to summarize at least one article located in the search. Arrange students into small groups to share their findings.
- Select a particular journal article that relates to a topic you are teaching. Generate some key terms associated with this topic with your students. Inform students of the general sense of the journal article and tell them to use the key terms and an appropriate database to locate the article. In the process of doing this they will find other papers that are relevant to the topic. Get them to summarize the article you specified and one other relevant article they found interesting. Arrange students into small groups to share their findings.
- When students are working on an assignment, get them to locate a specified number of references covering various aspects of the topic. Tell them to bring their print-outs to class and arrange them into small groups so that they can share them with fellow students. This will help expand the literature base available for the assignment.

Identifying main points from lectures and readings

Introduction

This is an important skill that students must possess if they are to learn effectively from lectures and readings. Students who cannot identify the main points will have difficulty understanding the content of lectures and readings, and will not be able to make appropriate notes from them.

Description

Identification of main points is based on three different sorts of knowledge.

Knowledge of the subject matter. Without some knowledge and understanding of the subject matter, it is difficult for students to determine what is important in a lecture or reading. In particular, students who are just beginning a new subject area are not usually able to decide which aspects of a theory are important (Shuell, 1990), and often make notes on inappropriate or unimportant information. As they gain experience with the subject matter they find it easier to decide what is important, and can be more selective about what they attend to.

Knowing the difference between general and specific ideas and between more inclusive and less inclusive ideas. This sort of knowledge helps students differentiate between the main points and ideas which are used to illustrate them.

Knowledge of the cues used to indicate main points. There are many cues that lecturers use to signal main points. For example, the lecturer might:

- use a different tone of voice
- repeat a point
- provide an example to illustrate a point
- pause to give students time to make notes
- point to an overhead transparency to highlight important points
- write on the whiteboard
- slow down for emphasis
- say 'there are three main reasons for this', or 'we'll look at this in more detail next week'.

In readings, important points may be indicated by using headings of various levels, by printing in bold type or italics, or by including the material in a chapter summary.

Teaching students to identify main points from lectures and readings

Time required: several sessions of about 15 minutes

Teaching students to identify main points involves developing their skills in each of the three types of knowledge we have identified.

Knowledge of the subject matter
Encourage students to do some pre-reading before they attend a lecture. This will give them an understanding of much of the new material that is presented in the lecture and make it easier for them to judge what is important. Students will find it helpful if you structure or guide their pre-reading in some way. For example you might suggest that students 'Find three reasons why...' or 'Provide an example from your own experience of...'. This will help them identify main points and differentiate them from information that illustrates or elaborates on the main points.

Knowing the difference between general and specific ideas and between more inclusive and less inclusive ideas
This will be facilitated if you:

- give students practice in arranging ideas in hierarchical order. Concept maps that require hierarchical arrangement of ideas are a useful way of developing this knowledge
- give students sets of concepts or terms relating to a particular topic, and get them to determine which ideas are more inclusive, and how each idea relates to the others
- work with selections from the textbook to differentiate between main points and details that develop these main points.

Knowledge of the cues used to indicate main points

This is easier to achieve with text than with lectures, since students can examine a chapter or a reading and identify the cues that the author used to draw attention to important points.

- Have students examine the various levels of headings used in a textbook or other reading, and point out that higher level headings are used for more inclusive ideas.
- Get students to identify how the author presents the main points: for example, in a topic sentence within a paragraph, or by elaborating with a margin note.

It is a little more difficult to teach students to identify main points in lectures, because there is usually no permanent record of the lecture. However, if you record a lecture you will be able to demonstrate the cues that lecturers use to highlight important points, and you can ask students to find examples of them in the lectures they attend. If you are giving the lecture yourself, you can tell students about the particular cues that you normally use and remind them of these cues during the lecture.

Using this process in class activities

After a lecture ask students to identify the most important points that were raised in the lecture and explain how they identified them as being the most important points. Put students into small groups to compare the points they noted with those noted by other students, and to explain and justify their selection.

Use a similar process to identify the main points of readings.

Other comments

Because students construct their own meaning of what they learn, you should expect that there will be some variation in what they identify as main points from their readings or lectures. This will probably be most obvious when they are in the early stages of learning a new subject area, since different students will bring different perspectives to the subject. As students become more experienced with the subject matter, you can expect them to reach more agreement about the main points.

Memorizing information

Introduction

Every subject area requires students to memorize information. However, since it is usually the meaning of the information that is important and not the particular way that it is expressed, most information does not have to be remembered verbatim. Learning and remembering the meaning of information is best done by focusing on understanding, and by engaging in activities that increase understanding, such as writing summaries in your own words, linking new ideas to established ideas, and trying to see the bigger picture. However, most subject areas contain some information that has to be memorized in the exact way that it is presented: for example, formulae in mathematics, chords in music, or vocabulary in a foreign language. A number of different memorization strategies can be used to help students remember this type of information.

Description

The strategies described in this section are used to remember information that has to be learned verbatim or in a specified order. They are not intended to be used with material that is to be learned with understanding and expressed in the students' own words.

Three types of strategies can be used to help memorize information: rehearsal, elaboration and organization.

Rehearsal is a powerful way of memorizing information and involves recalling the ideas that have to be learned and reciting them, either overtly or covertly. The process of trying to recite information from memory makes students revise and consolidate what they already know and indicates what information needs more practice.

Well established principles of rehearsal include the following (Eggen and Kauchak, 1992):

- memory for information improves with increasing amounts of rehearsal
- rehearsal spaced over time (distributed practice) is more effective than rehearsal that is concentrated (massed practice or cramming)
- active rehearsal (eg, recalling from memory without referring to notes) is more effective than passive rehearsal (eg, reading and re-reading notes).

Students can rehearse information whenever they have a few minutes of free time. If they write the information on cards and carry these cards with them, they can take out a card and practise recalling and reciting the relevant information. This uses the two processes of active rehearsal and distributed practice.

Elaboration involves linking ideas that have to be remembered with inform-ation that is already known. When it is used to remember information verbatim, it usually becomes a process of establishing meaningful connect-ions between ideas that are not normally associated with each other.

One example of the use of elaboration is the *keyword method* of learning vocabulary in a foreign language. This relies on imagery to establish a link between new information and what is already known. Students using this method would first choose a familiar English word that sounds like the foreign word. They would form a mental image that links the meaning of the foreign word with that of the English word. For example, the French word for a car's headlight is *phare*. This is pronounced like the English word 'far'. 'Far' becomes the keyword to which the French word *phare* is attached, and students imagine a car with its headlights projecting a beam of light 'far' ahead. Then when they have to remember the French equivalent of head-light, they think of the car projecting its headlights 'far' ahead, and respond with the French word *phare*.

Elaboration is also used with the *method of loci*, where students remember lists of unrelated items by imagining them being located in familiar locations in their home. This method is usually only appropriate for remembering information that has to be retained for a short period of time, for once a second list is learned, items in that list will displace items in the first list.

Some mnemonics provide another example of the use of elaboration. Mnemonics are an elaborative strategy in which the learner constructs a relationship between existing knowledge and information that has to be learned. In most mnemonics the relationship that is established is contrived rather than logical, yet well-constructed mnemonics can help students re-member information for long periods.

Organization involves grouping items that have to be remembered into logical categories. When the time comes to recall the items, students first recall the categories. They then find it easier to recall the individual items that belong to those categories. The process of grouping items into categories makes memorization easier because it provides a framework in which to locate and retrieve information, which reduces the overall demands placed on the student's memory.

For further details and examples of these memory strategies, see Eggen and Kauchak (1992) or Woolfolk (1993).

Teaching students memorization strategies

Time required: several sessions of about 15 minutes

The best way to help students improve their memory of subject matter is to help them learn it with understanding. However, there will be occasions when students have to memorize verbatim information that does not involve understanding. The strategies described in this section can be used to help them do this. The best time to present these strategies is when the subject matter you are teaching contains this type of information. Then you could do the following:

1. Identify an appropriate strategy for the particular information you are teaching (eg, an organizational, mnemonic or elaborative strategy).
2. Explain why the strategy works and describe how students can apply the strategy to learn the information. Let them practise using the strategy to learn the information.
3. Specify other information to be learned before the next class and ask students to use that strategy to help them learn this information.
4. In the next class get students to recall this information, and discuss how useful the strategy was in helping them learn it. Ask students to suggest other strategies that they could use to learn this information and discuss their relative effectiveness.
5. Ask students to consider other contexts and situations when it would be appropriate to use this strategy for remembering information.

Using these strategies in class activities

Arrange revision sessions when students have to recite information that they have memorized. Get them to share the strategies they used to remember the information and any mnemonics that they developed.

Arrange quizzes on important points, details and information, especially when you start a new topic or work with new vocabulary. Get successful students to describe the strategies they used to learn the information.

Caution

Overuse of these strategies is typical of students who adopt a surface approach to their learning. Make sure that students understand when it is appropriate to use these strategies for learning and remembering information. Discourage students from using them when they have to understand the information.

Note making for assignments

Introduction

When students prepare written assignments, they usually have to read relevant literature to find information on a particular question or topic. This type of reading is usually quite focused. It requires students to use an approach which is different from what they would use for other reading which is done for a less directed purpose. Accordingly the notes that students make should be different from those that they make in other circumstances.

Before using this strategy you should ensure that you are familiar with the process of 'Analysing a question and planning a response' presented in Chapter 9.

Description

After students have analysed an assignment topic and developed a plan that includes some fairly broad sections indicating the subject matter, we recommend that they use these section headings to arrange their notes. By doing this, their notes will be focused on the specific content area, and they will be less likely to make notes of irrelevant material.

Students should draw up one or more pages for each section heading. They should then divide each page into three columns: one for the main points, one for the development of the main points, and the third for the reference details. An example of this format is provided in Figure 7.1. In making notes they should start with one primary reference and work their way through it, looking for relevant ideas which they write on the appropriate notes page. When they have finished with this reference they should move on to another, looking only for new information which they enter on the relevant notes page. If they find information that has already been recorded they can either ignore it or add a brief annotation in the reference column indicating that another author has made the same point. This will help them balance their use of the various references.

After they have done this with a few references and find that they are not getting any new ideas, they should examine the notes they have made on each section to identify the points that they will use in the assignment. Each of these points will become a sub-section of the assignment or a major paragraph within it.

Making notes in this way will help students identify the main points they should make in the assignment, and will also give them enough detail to enable them to write from their notes without having to refer back to the readings. It also makes it easier for students to synthesize material from a variety of sources and to express their ideas in their own words.

Section topic:		

Main points	Development	Reference details

Figure 7.1 *Format for making notes for an assignment*

Teaching students to make notes for assignments

Time required: about 50 minutes

Most students will already have a particular way of reading the references required for an assignment and making notes from these readings. They may not heed suggestions that they should use a different approach unless they are convinced that it will work better for them. Therefore, there is little point in trying to teach them a new method until they indicate some dissatisfaction with their existing method. You can help them determine the effectiveness of their present note making methods by getting them to reflect on their experience of writing assignments and to identify aspects of their reading and note making skills that could be improved.

This strategy is best taught with reference to an assignment on which students are currently working. This is also the time when students are most likely to be conscious of any weaknesses in the approach they normally use to make notes for an assignment.

1. Get students to reflect on the process they normally use when reading and making notes for an assignment, and to identify how effective the process is for that purpose.
2. Explain the process described above, and use an overhead or chart to display the steps involved in making notes for an assignment. Encourage students to compare this process with the one they normally use.
3. Have students analyse the topic and do the preliminary planning (see 'Analysing a question and planning a response' in Chapter 9).
4. Model the process by using one of the readings suggested for the assignment.
5. Have students use the textbook or a primary reference to practise the skill.
6. When they have drawn up their notes, get them to work in small groups to compare the notes they have made. They should identify main and supporting points and discuss how these points address the assignment topic.
7. Get students to compare this note-making process with other processes they have used, and discuss how effective this process will be for assignments in other subject areas.

When students have submitted this particular assignment get them to reflect on how well this reading and note making process worked for them. (Refer to 'Learning from feedback' in Chapter 9 for suggestions on how to do this.)

Using this process in class activities

Select an important question or issue that you want students to discuss and, as a class activity, develop some section headings that are relevant to it (use the process described in the section 'Analysing a question and planning a response' in Chapter 9. Explain these section headings to the students and refer them to some relevant readings. Assign each student a particular section and appropriate reading, and have them make notes on their assigned sections before the next class. In the next class use the 'Jigsaw method' (see Chapter 11) to have the whole group develop an answer to the question.

Note making from lectures: following the lecturer's structure

Introduction

Effective note making from lectures does more than provide a record of the main points of the lecture. If students make their notes thoughtfully it will help them develop a better understanding of the subject matter, especially if they actively relate new ideas to their existing knowledge (Peper and Mayer, 1986). Their learning will also be enhanced if they write notes in their own words instead of just copying down the lecturer's words or transcribing information from overheads.

There are several ways of structuring notes made during lectures. However, when students attend a lecture without any prior knowledge of what will be covered, it is usually best for them to make their notes by following the sequence of ideas used by the lecturer. The format presented here was adapted from the note taking scheme developed by Jeanette Lawrence (Lawrence and Chalmers, 1989; Lawrence *et al.*, 1989).

Description

There are two main considerations in making notes using the lecturer's structure:

- deciding what material is important enough to note
- recording this information.

Deciding what is important requires students to listen actively for the main points of the lecture, including important facts, principles and generalizations. Students need to make sure that they do not confuse important principles and generalizations with the details that are used to illustrate them. Some cues which will help students focus on important matters include verbal cues such as 'there are three reasons for this', and non-verbal cues such as the lecturer emphasizing particular words or pointing to items on an overhead. While these cues may seem obvious, students who are unfamiliar with lectures may not be aware of them. Further information on this matter is presented in 'Identifying main points from lectures and readings' earlier in this chapter.

It is important for students to prepare for a lecture even when they intend to use the lecturer's structure for making notes. One way of doing this is to review notes they have made in previous classes and complete any suggested preliminary reading. By doing this, they will get a sense of what the lecture will be about and will become familiar with some of the new terms that will be used. This will make it easier for them to identify the main points of the lecture.

As well as identifying what information they should note, students have to actually make the notes about this information. Effective lecture notes include the following features:

- clear provision for recording the main points of the lecture
- provision for examples, illustrations or development of the main points to be written near the main points
- space where students can write a summary of the lecture
- space where students can add extra details when they read set readings, complete class exercises and review their notes.

Figure 7.2 provides a format for making lecture notes that have these features.

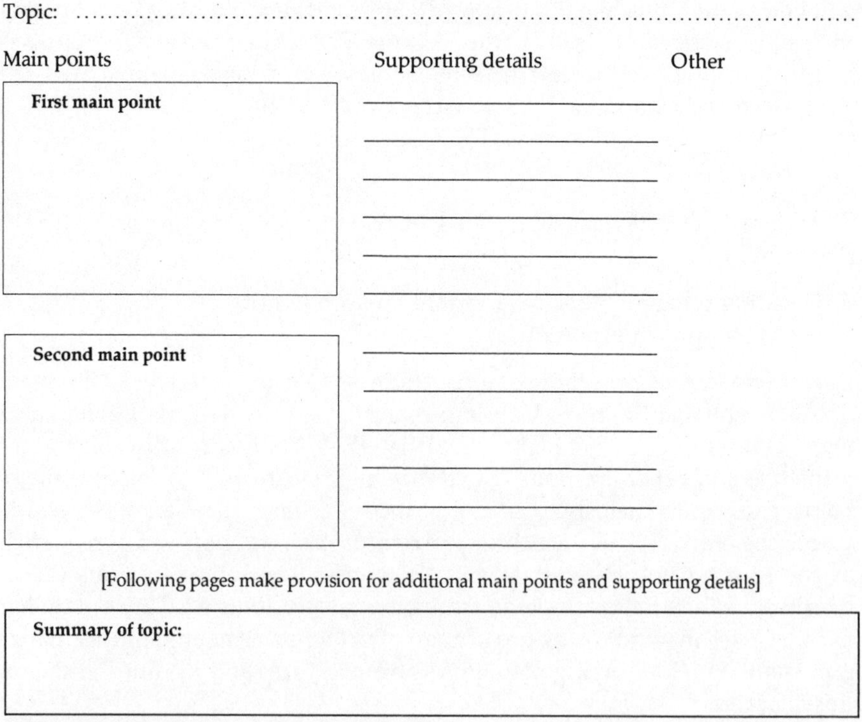

Topic: ....

Main points	Supporting details	Other
First main point		
Second main point		

[Following pages make provision for additional main points and supporting details]

Summary of topic:

Figure 7.2 *Format for lecture notes*

Students should review their lecture notes promptly after the lecture while the content is fresh in their minds so that they can clarify points they did not understand and add details they missed. They should also write a brief summary of the lecture. This will consolidate their understanding of the lecture and provide a useful resource they can use when revising the topic at a later date.

We do not normally advise students to tape-record lectures; it is usually wasteful of student time because they have to listen to the full lecture again. It also postpones the process of listening actively to the lecture and working out its main points. We believe it is better for students to listen actively while the lecture is being delivered, and correct any gaps in their notes by checking with a fellow student or by finding the information in their readings.

Teaching students to make notes from lectures

Time required: two sessions, each of about 20 minutes

Most students are familiar with the process of making notes by following the lecturer's structure. However, many students have difficulty working out the main points of a lecture, and copy down much of it word for word, regardless of its importance. One of the biggest challenges in teaching students to make notes effectively is to get them to focus on main points rather than details.

Before teaching students how to make notes from lectures, make a set of notes from a recent lecture that the students have attended. Put these notes on an overhead transparency.

1. Introduce note making by having students examine the notes they made in the recent lecture and use them to write a summary of the main ideas presented in the lecture. Get them to compare their notes and summary with those of a partner, and determine how adequate their notes were as a basis for writing a summary.
2. Discuss the importance of making good notes from lectures, and explain the features of an effective note-making system. Get students to analyse their own notes in terms of these features.
3. Explain when it is appropriate to make notes using the lecturer's structure.
4. Display the notes that you made from the lecture and explain how you decided what information was important enough to note. Also explain the features of the format you used to set out your notes. Indicate how you leave space in the notes to add information from readings and other sources. Give students an opportunity to discuss the notes you made and compare them with those they made from the same lecture.
5. Ask students to use the lecturer's structure to make notes at their next lecture. You should plan to attend this lecture and make notes from it.
6. After the next lecture have students work in pairs to compare their notes and explain to their partner why they thought each point was important

enough to note. They should also compare the format they used to write their notes and the summary they made of the lecture.

7. Display the notes you made on this lecture and the summary paragraph you wrote, and invite discussion.

8. Get students to consider when it would be appropriate to make notes in this way and discuss how useful this approach would be in other courses they are studying.

There will be times when students find it difficult to make notes in this way. For example, some lectures are presented in a way that makes it difficult for students to differentiate between main points and supporting ideas. When this happens, students have to choose between persisting with the method and perhaps missing some important information or copying everything down without separating main points from supporting ideas. One way of handling this situation is for them to copy down as much as possible, and then write the notes properly after the lecture. Students are less likely to experience this difficulty if they prepare for the lecture by doing some preliminary reading.

Students are more likely to use this method if they are convinced that it overcomes difficulties they have experienced with note making. You might be able to demonstrate this by getting them to write a summary of a topic based on the notes they made with this method, and then compare it with a summary of a different topic based on notes they made with their previous method. They should notice an improvement in the quality of their summaries. This can be attributed both to the better quality of their notes and to the increased understanding of the topic which occurs when they make notes in this way.

Using lecture notes in class activities

Get students to work in pairs to compare the notes they made from a lecture and their summaries of the lecture. This will enhance their understanding of the lecture and provide feedback about their note making and summarizing skills.

After a lecture, get students to review their notes in class and add relevant material from their textbook or other readings. This will give them an opportunity to review the content of the lecture while it is fresh in their minds and link it to information contained in their readings.

Other matters

If you think the lecturer will accept the feedback, ask your students to identify what the lecturer could have done to make it easier for them to make notes from that lecture. Pass on any worthwhile suggestions to the lecturer.

Note making from lectures: using a structure developed from prior reading

Introduction

Effective note making from lectures does more than provide a record of the main points of the lecture. If students make their notes thoughtfully it will help them develop a better understanding of the subject matter, especially if they actively relate new ideas to their existing knowledge (Peper and Mayer, 1986). Their learning will also be enhanced if they write notes in their own words instead of just copying down the lecturer's words or transcribing from overheads.

Structuring lecture notes on the basis of prior reading has distinct advantages. Since students do some prior reading and make notes on it before class, they will come to the lecture with some knowledge of what points are important and how ideas relate to each other. Then it will be easier for them to decide what points in the lecture are important enough to note. Furthermore, since they have already made some notes from their reading they will not have to make as many notes during the lecture. Therefore they will have more time to listen and think about the material that is being presented. Another advantage of using this approach is that students will have one set of notes that integrates information obtained from the lecture with that obtained from the readings.

Description

1. Prior to the lecture, students read the text and other appropriate readings on the topic. They make notes from these readings, leaving plenty of space between the main points so that additional material can be added during the lecture. They should also leave space where they can write a summary of the lecture.
2. In the lecture, students listen for new material and add it in an appropriate space in their notes. This new material may comprise new points which did not occur in the readings, or the development of points already noted.
3. After the lecture, students should review their notes promptly while the content is fresh in their minds so they can clarify points they did not understand and add details they missed. They should also write a brief summary of the lecture. This will consolidate their understanding of the lecture and will be useful for revision.

Teaching students to make notes on the basis of prior reading

Time required: two sessions; one about 15 minutes, the other about 20 minutes

Most students prefer to make notes using the lecturer's structure. One of the challenges in teaching students to structure lecture notes on their reading is to convince them that they will not miss any important information presented in the lecture. Another challenge is to convince them that the time spent in doing the preliminary reading and making notes from it is time well spent. The following procedure specifically addresses these concerns.

1. Before teaching this process, use it to make a set of notes from a recent lecture that the students have attended. Write your notes on an overhead transparency in two colours. Use one colour for the notes you made from the readings, and a different colour for the notes you added during the lecture.
2. Explain the process of making notes in this way, pointing out the advantages of using this approach and addressing the concern that students have about missing important points.
3. Display the notes you made from the lecture and readings, and use them to illustrate the features of the method. Show that this approach reduced the amount of notes made during the lecture. This will be easy to demonstrate if you have written them in different colours.
4. Ask the students to make notes in this way at the next lecture, using different colours for the notes made from reading and those made in the lecture. Give them some guidance about which are the most relevant readings for this purpose, and how they could structure the notes they make from these readings.
5. After the next lecture get students to work in pairs or small groups to compare their notes and summary statements and explain why they selected particular points as being important.
6. Display your own notes and summary, and invite students to discuss them.
7. Ask students to consider the advantages and disadvantages of using this approach to making notes compared with other approaches they have used.
8. Get students to consider when it is appropriate to make notes in this way and how useful the approach would be in other courses they are studying.

Students will only use this method if they are convinced that it is better than the method they normally use. You may be able to demonstrate this by getting them to write a summary of a topic based on the notes they made from a lecture with this method, and compare it with a summary of a different topic based on notes they made in another lecture with their previous method. Students should notice an improvement in the quality of their summaries. This can be attributed both to the better quality of their notes and to their better understanding of the topic.

Using lecture notes in class activities

Get students to work in pairs or small groups to compare the notes they made from a lecture and the summaries they wrote. This will enhance their understanding of the lecture and provide feedback about their note making and summarizing skills.

Other matters

Many students are reluctant to use this approach and prefer to follow the lecturer's structure; they fear that they will overlook some important points in the lecture. You should reassure them that if they make notes in this way they will actually have more time in the lecture to work out what is important. Furthermore, if you make a practice of getting students to review the main points of the lecture in the next class, they will be able to add any important points they have missed.

If you think the lecturer will accept the feedback, ask your students to identify what the lecturer could have done to make it easier for them to make notes from that lecture. Pass on any worthwhile suggestions to the lecturer.

Note making from text

Introduction

Effective note making involves more than just recording the main points of a reading. It requires students to determine what their purpose is in reading the text, and what information is relevant to that purpose. It gives them practice in working out the main points of the reading. Furthermore, if students write the notes in their own words instead of copying directly from the text, they develop a better understanding of the text they are studying (Wittrock, 1990).

Description

The procedure that we recommend for making notes from text is based on processes followed by skilled note takers (Lawrence *et al.*, 1989) and is adapted from a note taking scheme developed by Jeanette Lawrence (Lawrence and Chalmers, 1989). It includes activities that help students to understand the overall meaning of the reading as well as to record the details of its various sections. The resulting notes are arranged in a way that makes it easy for students to find information at different levels, and to differentiate between the main ideas and examples that illustrate these main ideas.

The method involves the following steps:

1. Students prepare pages on which to write their notes (see the format provided in Figure 7.3).
2. On the first page, they complete the bibliographic details of the reading.
3. They skim read the whole text to get a general idea of what it is about (see 'Skim reading text' later in this chapter). They should not make any notes at this stage. When they have done this they write a sentence describing what the reading is about, and put it in the box headed 'About 1', on the first page (see Figure 7.3).
4. Students then work on the paragraphs or sections of the text one at a time, as follows:
   - They read each paragraph or section, and then use their own words to write a short summary statement that describes its main idea. They put this under the 'Paragraph/Section' heading. They should also record the number of the page from which the information was taken.
   - They work out the main points in the paragraph or section that elaborate on this main idea, and list them in the 'Points' column alongside that main idea. Again, they should use their own words. If there is anything they do not understand or if there are questions they want to follow up, they should list them in the 'Extras' column.
5. When they have done this for each paragraph or section, they quickly re-read the whole article and, in the box headed 'About 2', write a second brief summary of what it is about. They compare what they have written in the two 'About' boxes to see how much their understanding of the article changed after the detailed reading.

Students now have a detailed summary of the text that contains the main ideas and some specific points that expand on them. When students have to revise the topic or write an assignment on it, they should not have to refer back to the original text unless they have a different purpose from that which originally applied. This makes their assignment writing and revision much more efficient.

In addition to having a useful set of notes, students will also have a reasonable understanding of the content of the text. Achieving this level of understanding is one of the major benefits of making notes in this way.

Reference details: ....

About 1:

**Main idea of paragraph
or section**   **Supporting details**   **Extras**

First paragraph or section:	

Second paragraph or section:	

[Following pages make provision for additional main points and supporting details.
The last page also contains the About 2 box.]

About 2:

Figure 7.3 *Format for notes made from text*

Teaching note making

Time required: about 45 minutes

Students will already have their preferred ways of making notes from text, and many of them are likely to be reasonably satisfied with the particular methods they use. They may not heed suggestions that they should use a different approach unless they are convinced that it will work better for them. Therefore there is little point in trying to teach them a new method until they indicate some dissatisfaction with existing methods. You can help them determine the effectiveness of their present note making methods by getting them to use their notes as a basis for completing a significant task, such as writing a summary of a topic or writing an answer to an examination question. If their notes are inadequate for the purpose, students are more likely to be interested in learning about a different note making method.

The following procedure for teaching students how to make notes assumes that they are aware that their present methods have some limitations, and that they are willing to try a different method.

1. Get students to identify the limitations of their present methods of making notes from text.
2. Explain the steps involved in the note making method described in this section. Display them on an overhead or chart. Explain why this is an efficient way to make notes from text, and how it overcomes the difficulties they have identified in their present methods.
3. Select an appropriate section of the textbook or a reading that relates to a topic that you are currently teaching, and model the process of making notes from it. As you use each step, refer students to the overhead or chart. When modelling the process, make sure that you think aloud about how you decide what is important and worthy of noting.
4. Give the class another section to practise on. Leave the overhead or chart displayed. While they are doing this, make your own notes for this section on an overhead or chart.
5. Arrange students into pairs to compare the notes they have taken. In doing this they should explain why they selected particular points as being the most important or most noteworthy. They should also explain how these notes differ from those they normally make.
6. Display the notes you have just made on this reading, and discuss any differences between your notes and those made by the students.
7. Assign students a particular reading and tell them to make notes from this reading and bring them to the next class.
8. In the next class, repeat steps 5 and 6.
9. Get students to consider when it would be appropriate to make notes in this way and whether they could use this method in other courses they are studying.

Students are more likely to use this method if they are convinced that it overcomes difficulties they previously experienced with note making. You may be able to demonstrate this by getting them to write a summary of a topic based on the notes they made from a reading using this method, and to compare it with a summary of a different topic based on notes they made using their previous method. Students should notice an improvement in the quality of their summaries. This can be attributed both to the better quality of their notes and to their better understanding of the topic.

Once students have learned to make notes in this way, they may wish to modify some feature of the process. You should not discourage them from doing this, provided they do not abandon a feature that is essential to learning with understanding. For example, while it might be appropriate to make some formatting changes to the notes page, it would not be appropriate for them to abandon the process of writing the summary statements of what the reading is about. Nor would it be appropriate for students to make notes verbatim using the author's words instead of writing them in their own words.

Using notes made from text in class activities

Notes that students have made from their reading can be used in a variety of class activities that involve writing. For example, you could get students to use their notes to write a paragraph on a specified topic. This will help develop their understanding of the topic and also develop their writing skills. You could also get them to use their notes as a basis for writing an answer to a practice examination question. This will give them feedback on how adequate their notes are for this purpose as well as giving them practice in preparing for examinations.

Other comments

Some students will find it difficult to make notes in this way, especially if they usually just highlight sections of the text or copy information verbatim from the text. You will have to work with them to convince them that the extra effort is worthwhile.

This method of making notes works well with text that is clearly structured in a linear fashion. When you are teaching students how to use this method, make sure that you start with sections of text that will be fairly easy for them to work on.

Encourage students to adapt the notes page to suit their particular needs. However, discourage them from making adaptations that reduce the amount of thought that they use in making their notes.

Skim reading

Introduction

Skim reading enables students to find out quickly what a text is about. They can then judge whether it is worth spending more time reading it in detail. In this respect, skilful skim reading helps students use their study time more efficiently. However, it does more than this. If students skim read an article or chapter before they study it in detail, they will become familiar with its content and structure and be able to relate it to relevant material that they already know about the topic. When they come to study the text in detail, it will be easier for them to identify the main points and select the most significant supporting details.

Description

The following description of skim reading is related to reading a chapter from a conventional textbook. The chapter will probably have an introduction, followed by subject matter arranged in sections. These sections may be divided into subsections and may include illustrations, tables or graphs. At the end of the chapter there will probably be a conclusion. There may also be a summary and a glossary of important terms. We encourage students to follow these steps:

1. Read the introduction carefully to find out what the chapter is about.
2. Reflect on what they already know about the topic and recall any relevant information or ideas.
3. Look at the highest level section headings presented in the chapter and try to work out what each section might be about. If a section contains an introductory paragraph, read this thoughtfully. Then look at the lower level section headings, which will help them work out what the chapter is about. If there are any illustrations or graphs they should examine them and try to work out what they mean.
4. When they have done this for all sections, they should read the conclusion and summary. If there is a glossary of terms presented at the end of the chapter, they should look through it to identify the key terms that are used. This will indicate those ideas in the chapter they already know something about.

Students should now be able to explain briefly what the chapter is about and decide whether it is worth reading in more detail. If they decide to read in more detail and make notes from the reading, they should begin by writing a brief explanation of what it is about in the 'About 1' box on their notes page (see 'Note making from text' earlier in this chapter). Apart from this, we suggest that they do not make any notes as they skim read.

The process of skim reading other forms of text such as journal articles is similar.

Teaching skim reading

Time required: about 45 minutes

Some students are more attracted to the way that skim reading can help them save time than to its use in helping them understand a reading. When you are teaching them how to skim read, you should stress both functions and emphasize that skim reading requires readers to *work at* understanding the text. This takes more effort than just looking through the text and marking it with a highlighting pen.

1. Explain the purposes of skim reading. Get students to indicate what they currently do to achieve these purposes and examine how effective this is.
2. Explain the steps involved in skim reading. Display them on an overhead or chart. Explain that skilful skim reading is an effective way of previewing a reading, and indicate how it overcomes weaknesses they identified in their present methods.
3. Select an appropriate chapter of a textbook and model the process of skim reading it. As you do this, refer students to the specific steps presented on the overhead or chart. Make sure that you think aloud about how you decide what to focus on, and how you recall and use your existing knowledge. Conclude by constructing one or two sentences that summarize what the chapter is about.
4. Give students another chapter to practise on. Leave the overhead or chart displayed. Tell them to write one or two sentences summarizing what the chapter is about.
5. Arrange students into pairs or small groups to share their understanding of what they have read. The main purpose of this is for them to realize how much they can get from a brief survey of the text, provided they do it thoughtfully.
6. Get students to discuss circumstances when it is appropriate to skim read sections of text, and to consider how they can use this process in other courses they are studying.

Using skim reading in class activities

Before you teach a new topic in class, ask students to skim read the relevant section of their textbook. This will get them ready to work with the new ideas you present in class as well as giving them practice in the process of skim reading.

Chapter 8:

Strategies for Working with Information

The strategies presented in this chapter are used to increase understanding of information that has been learned. They require students to recall and use information, to focus on main points, to organize information and link it with what they already know. One or two of the strategies (eg, writing paragraphs) might seem to involve only general writing skills. However this is not the case. Writing a paragraph requires students to differentiate between main points and supporting details, and to make links between the ideas presented in that paragraph and adjacent paragraphs.

These strategies can be used by individuals working alone. However they are more effective when students work in small groups, for this stimulates interaction between students that is purposeful and focused on particular aspects of the subject matter. In Part One we argued that understanding is socially constructed, and working in small groups provides an opportunity for students to develop their understanding in this way.

Students who adopt a surface approach to their learning tend not to use these strategies. If you are teaching students who are accustomed to using surface strategies, you will probably have to convince them that they will benefit from putting in the effort needed to work with information instead of just completing the task in the easiest way.

- Explaining ideas
- Generating questions
- Making concept maps
- Organizing ideas

- Using a systematic approach to learning
- Using study groups
- Writing paragraphs
- Writing summaries from notes

Explaining ideas

Introduction

The ability to explain one's ideas, beliefs and perspectives is an important life skill, as well as being important in class activities such as seminars and tutorials. Having students explain their understanding or beliefs is a powerful way of helping them clarify their thinking and monitor their understanding of the topic (Pressley *et al.*, 1992; Webb, 1989). Most students are probably more practised in giving explanations than they realize, since there are many informal occasions when they explain things to other people. However, explaining their ideas about subject matter is often more demanding, and many students are unclear about the components of an effective explanation of subject matter.

Description

Barry and King (1993, p.531) describe several characteristics of an effective explanation:

- the new information is matched to the receiver's present knowledge
- the presentation is structured to provide a preview, regular summaries, and a final review
- the information is sequenced in a way that facilitates learning, typically by gradually increasing the difficulty or complexity of the material
- general principles are illustrated by using specific examples or analogies
- the material is presented in an appropriate way. For spoken explanations this refers to such matters as volume, pacing and articulation.

If students are to develop the skill of explaining, they need to be able to explain their ideas to somebody else and then receive feedback on the quality of their explanation. It is usually better for them to do this in fairly small groups. Groups of three are particularly effective because each person can be actively involved at all times, with one person explaining, another listening to the explanation and the third person giving feedback about the quality of the explanation.

Some principles which should be followed when students are explaining their ideas in this way include:

- students need to be given sufficient time to plan the explanation
- they should be encouraged to explain ideas in their own words instead of using the textbook or lecturer's words
- they should use vocabulary that is appropriate to the subject area
- they should illustrate general ideas and principles with examples, diagrams, etc.
- they should provide opportunities for others to ask questions and clarify their understanding.

Teaching students to explain their ideas

Time required: about 40 minutes

1. Explain the characteristics of an effective explanation and illustrate them with appropriate examples. Display these characteristics on an overhead transparency or chart.
2. Select three important topics that have already been covered in the course. Arrange students in threes and instruct each student to take one of the topics and plan how to explain this topic to the group.
3. Get students to present their explanations to the group. One person acts as the explainer, a second as the receiver, while the third acts as an observer who gives feedback on the explanation. Students take turns at presenting their explanations, and then rotate the roles so that each takes a turn as an explainer, a receiver and an observer.
4. Ask students to consider how they could use the skill of explaining in other courses they are studying and in private study groups.

Using explaining in class activities

Explaining activities can be used in most classes and with most topics. It does not take much time and provides an opportunity for students to consolidate their understanding of important ideas. Whenever an opportunity arises, have students plan an explanation and present it to a partner.

Another way to practise this skill and develop students' understanding of key terms is to present students with a list of key terms at the end of a class and ask them to prepare brief explanations of each term. In the next class arrange them into small groups so that they can explain the key terms and obtain feedback about the quality of their explanations.

Generating questions

Introduction

Skill in questioning is an important component in monitoring one's progress in learning. However, most students are more accustomed to answering questions than asking them. Some students may ask themselves questions about the subject matter when they are revising for examinations, but they do not usually do this in the earlier stages of a course. It is important for students to ask questions about the subject matter even in the early stages of learning, for this will encourage them to think about the subject matter and relate new ideas to what they already know. It will also help them develop an inquiring approach to their learning.

Questions generated by students can be used in class activities to enhance learning and understanding of the subject matter. Small group activities that involve students in answering thought-provoking questions generated by their peers have been shown to have a significant effect on their learning (King, 1990).

Description

Questions can be worded to enable students to explore various levels of learning, such as knowledge of the subject matter, understanding of it, or ability to think about it. Although all these levels are important, students often focus on details and overlook the higher levels when they question themselves on the subject matter.

One way of helping students ask higher level questions is to get them to use *generic question stems* that can be developed into specific questions. The following stems have been shown to be effective in promoting higher level questioning (King, 1992). Students use the stems to prepare specific questions about the particular subject matter they are studying.

What is a new example of...?
How would you use... to...?
What would happen if...?
What are the strengths and weaknesses of...?
What do we already know about...?
How does... relate to what we learned before about...?
Explain why...
Explain how...
How does... affect...?
What is the meaning of...?
Why is... important?
What is the difference between... and...?

How are... and... similar?
What is the best... and why is it the best?
What are some possible solutions for...?
Compare... and... with respect to...
What causes...?

Teaching students to generate questions

Time required: about 30 minutes

1. Explain the importance of student generated questions in learning and how they can help students understand the subject matter.
2. Explain the purpose of the generic question stems.
3. Select a particular topic that you have been teaching and demonstrate how to use the generic stems to form specific questions about the topic.
4. Tell the students to form some questions about current subject matter. Many students have difficulty doing this, so be prepared to give them help with this task. Emphasize that they should not just prepare questions to which they already know the answer, and that they should include questions which do not have an obvious answer.
5. Arrange students into pairs or small groups to ask and answer the questions they have prepared.
6. Select one or two questions for discussion on a whole-class basis.
7. Get students to consider the importance of generating questions in other courses they are studying, and to discuss how they could use these question stems in their own study and with study groups.

Using student generated questions in class activities

List some important terms or concepts from the subject matter you are teaching. Ask students to prepare some questions about these terms, and then work with a partner or small group to answer the questions.

Revise previous topics by getting students to prepare questions and work with a partner or small group to answer them. Class time can be saved if students prepare the questions before class.

Assign some reading to be done before the next class, and ask students to prepare some questions on this reading. Start the class by getting students to work together to answer their questions.

At the end of a class, ask students to generate some questions on that topic. Select some of the better questions and get students to prepare answers to them for the next class. In the next class, arrange students into small groups to discuss their answers.

Select some of the questions that students have prepared and use them in a revision quiz.

Making concept maps

Introduction

In order for students to learn with understanding they must link together the various components of the subject matter, and relate them to ideas from other topics and to their own experience. Concept maps provide a diagrammatic representation of these links (Novak and Gowin, 1984). They can be used for a number of purposes (Pauk, 1989), such as to:

- summarize ideas from a textbook that students want to understand thoroughly
- organize sets of ideas that are complex and difficult to understand
- clarify passages of text that are not well written
- summarize lecture notes
- organize ideas for writing essays or making speeches
- review for examinations.

These maps are informative to the teacher, who can compare the relationships with those that a subject matter expert might make. They are also informative to students, for they can indicate strengths and weaknesses in their understanding. They provide this information efficiently, for experienced students can usually produce a concept map more quickly than they can write an essay.

Figures 8.1 and 8.2 are examples of concept maps. We prepared them by mapping the names of some familiar animals. In the first map we arranged the animals according to their biological classification; in the second we arranged them in terms of whether the animals are domestic or untamed, and then subdivided them into other categories. Both maps provide a clear picture of relationships that we identified between these terms. Since the maps are supposed to show how people structure their knowledge, neither map is more correct than the other. If you have a preference for one map over the other it is probably because it is closer to your own way of arranging these ideas.

Description

Concept mapping involves the following steps:

1. Identify the ideas or terms to be mapped.
2. Write each idea on a small card or piece of paper. Post-its are convenient for this.
3. Arrange the cards in a way that makes most sense to you. Place ideas that are closely related near one other. What 'closely related' actually means is decided by the person doing the mapping.

4. Draw lines between ideas that are related, and write on each line a phrase identifying the nature of the relationship. This is important because it makes you clarify the relationships that you see between the various ideas.

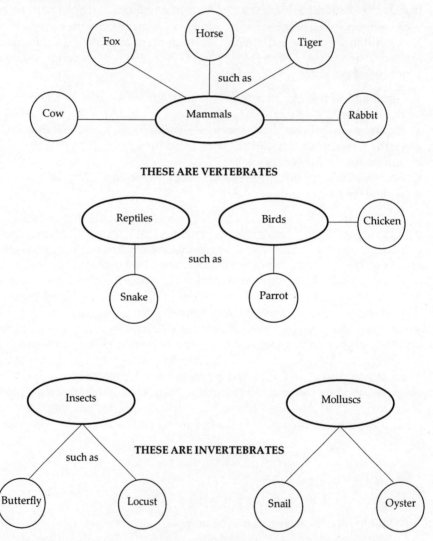

Figure 8.1 *Concept map 1 – animals arranged according to their biological classification*

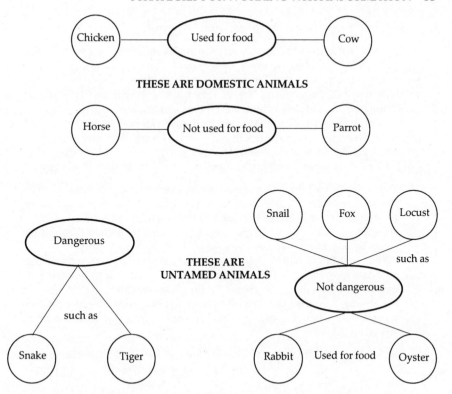

Figure 8.2 *Concept map 2 – animals arranged according to familiarity and use*

Teaching concept mapping

Time required: about 40 minutes

1. Explain the purpose of concept mapping.
2. Select about ten familiar terms or items and model the process of mapping them. When modelling, think aloud about alternative ways that you could arrange the terms.
3. Give students a similar number of terms from the subject matter that they have been studying and get them to work in small groups to map the terms. While they are doing this, move between groups and ask them to explain the linkages they have identified.
4. Select one or two groups to display their maps to the rest of the class and explain the linkages they identified.
5. Get students to consider how they could use concept mapping in other courses they are studying, both in their private study and with study groups.

Using concepts maps in class activities

When you teach a new topic, get students to map some terms selected from that topic and from other topics that you have taught. You might also include some terms taught in other courses. This will encourage students to make associations between the topics covered in the various courses. It will also give you an indication of how well they understand the subject matter.

Towards the end of the semester, get students to identify and map the most important terms presented during the semester. This can be a powerful review process. It can be done individually, in small groups or on a whole-class basis. We have used it as a class activity at the end of semester in the following way:

1. Get students individually to select about five important terms presented during the semester and write a brief explanation of each term. If necessary, they should refer to their textbook and notes while doing this.
2. Arrange students into small groups to clarify their understanding of these terms by questioning and explaining.
3. Working with the whole class, construct a concept map of the terms that students have identified. Do this by asking students in turn to contribute one term, which they first explain to the class and then indicate where it fits among the terms that have already been mapped. Do not locate the term in the map until there is general agreement about where it should be placed.

Students report that this activity clarifies their understanding of the various terms and their relationship with other important ideas presented in the course.

Organizing ideas

Introduction

Effective learning and understanding requires students to organize subject matter in a coherent way. Proper organization makes it easier to learn material and recall it later. In most university courses subject matter is broken up into discrete topics. Even though lecturers are aware of the structure of the discipline and the linkages between the various topics, they do not always make these clear to students. Some students may complete a course of study without ever becoming aware of the way that important ideas are related. So, unless deliberate attempts are made to encourage students to make links between these ideas, many of them will learn the subject matter in a fragmented way and will not understand it properly.

Description

A simple means of organizing ideas is to use a matrix or table that provides headings under which information can be arranged. For example, in a course on human development our students organized their knowledge of physical development in the following one-page matrix:

Age	Characteristics of this age	Implications for teachers
3–5 years		
6–12 years		
13–17 years		

Students completed similar matrices for other aspects of development, such as social, moral and cognitive development. In order to complete the matrices, students had to identify differences in development between the specified age groups and think about the implications of these differences for teachers. When they had completed all the matrices, students pasted them together to produce a summary of the major areas of development at the various age levels. The process helped them organize information that they otherwise might have learned just as a series of discrete and unrelated items. It also helped them see how this information could be applied to classroom teaching.

Teaching students to organize ideas

Time required: about 30 minutes

1. Select a topic that has been covered recently in class. Work with the students on a whole-class basis to identify headings that could be used to organize information about this topic.
2. Draw up a table that uses these headings and demonstrate how to use it by completing one or two cells. Have students work in small groups to complete the rest of the table.
3. Encourage groups to share completed tables with other groups or the whole class.

4. Get students to describe and evaluate other ways they use to organize information.
5. Have students reflect on the importance of organizing information for other topics and in other subjects they are taking. Discuss some organizing themes that they could use in these situations. Also get students to consider how they could use this process in study groups.

Using this process in class activities

As well as giving students pre-reading to do before class, give them a set of categories into which you want them to arrange the ideas that are contained in the reading. In the next class put them in groups to discuss how they categorized the information from the reading.

With some preliminary planning, the process of organizing ideas in a matrix can be used to help students build up a summary of main ideas on a week-by-week basis. For example, in the course on human development that we referred to earlier, we asked students to prepare a summary chart each week on one of the major areas of development such as cognitive development, social development and moral development. At the end of the semester they pasted these charts together so that they had a comprehensive summary of the main features of human development and their implications for teachers.

Using a matrix to organize ideas can also be used to help students survey a topic before they study it in detail. Display the matrix on an overhead transparency and work with the class to enter important ideas and information in the various cells. Even with a new topic students will usually be able to provide enough information to allow you to make an entry in each cell of the matrix. Students can expand these entries after more detailed study of the topic. For example, if you were going to examine the use of particular types of test items used in university examinations, you might work with a matrix like the following:

	Essay items	Multiple-choice items
Characteristics		
Strengths		
Weaknesses		
Appropriate conditions for use		

Using a systematic approach to learning

Introduction

We believe that if students are systematic in the way they approach their learning, they will understand the subject matter better and be more successful with their studies.

Description

We have adapted a simple problem-solving strategy that involves four components (Polya, 1957):

- Identify the nature of the task or problem.
- Plan a sequence of steps to complete the task or develop a solution to the problem.
- Implement these steps and monitor progress.
- Check the final solution to ensure that all task requirements have been met.

Although these components are presented in a particular order, they are not steps that must be followed in that order. In most situations, working on one component provides information about the others, and students typically find themselves moving backwards and forwards from one to another.

Teaching students to use a systematic approach to learning

Time required: about 20 minutes, with brief follow-ups

We have found that this process cannot be taught on a single occasion. Although it is easy for students to learn the components of the strategy, it usually takes some time for them to apply it to their learning. Therefore it is necessary to remind them about the strategy and to model its use regularly.

When you introduce the strategy you should relate it to a significant activity in which students are engaged, such as managing their reference reading, writing an assignment or preparing for a test or examination. In the steps below, we have related it to an assignment:

1. Explain the components of the strategy and have students relate them to their own experience.
2. Get students to identify the requirements of the assignment and plan what they will do in order to complete it.
3. In the next few classes encourage students to monitor their progress by having them identify the activities they have completed and those that require further work. Where appropriate get them to revise their plans for writing the assignment.

4. Use the strategy with other class activities so that students experience it being used in a variety of situations. Get feedback from students about its effectiveness in helping them go about their learning in a systematic way.
5. Have students reflect on the use of the strategy for other tasks and in other courses they are studying.

Using study groups

Introduction

Sharing ideas with others is an effective way to enhance learning. Students can do this in their own time if they set up study groups which work on various aspects of the course content. These study groups allow students to work on topics of their own choice and reduce their dependence on the lecturer. They can provide emotional support and encouragement to students who are experiencing difficulty. They also provide an opportunity for students to develop and improve learning strategies such as questioning, explaining and summarizing.

Description

There are many activities that students can use in study groups, including:

- asking and answering questions
- reading each other's work
- explaining ideas to the group
- presenting summaries of readings
- solving problems in a collaborative way
- determining important points in a topic
- analysing case studies
- debating a topic
- preparing for examinations.

Encouraging students to use study groups

Time required: no specific requirement, for this is treated incidentally

Students sometimes need encouragement to establish and use study groups. You can help them by engaging in activities such as the following:

- discuss what students can gain from using study groups

- give students permission to use a classroom as a meeting place
- explain and demonstrate activities that can be used by study groups
- suggest specific activities that are relevant to topics you are currently teaching
- make yourself available to help students in their groups
- establish a way for students to contact each other outside class
- arrange a schedule of tutorless tutorials where students can work on topics that you have developed.

Students who are accustomed to a system that emphasizes individual effort and promotes competition between students may not be comfortable working with study groups, and may feel that there is an element of collusion involved. If you wish to encourage them to use student study groups it will be necessary to address their concerns explicitly.

Using study groups in class activities

There are several class activities you can use which will encourage students to establish study groups and work effectively in them. For example:

- when you get students to work in small groups in class, allow them to work with their study group
- invite study groups to raise questions that arose in their groups, and spend class time considering these questions
- invite groups to prepare and deliver answers to questions that you raise in class.

Writing paragraphs

Introduction

Writing paragraphs is an important component of academic writing. Many students are not skilled at this, and write single sentence paragraphs or paragraphs that lack coherence. Teaching them to write paragraphs on the subject matter they are studying will increase their understanding of the subject matter (Wittrock, 1990) as well as improve their writing skills.

Description

In academic writing, a paragraph consists of the expression of a main idea and some elaboration of this idea. This may involve an explanation, some supporting evidence or an example. The main idea is expressed in a topic sentence and the elaboration is expressed in a number of supporting sentences. The topic sentence is often the first sentence in the paragraph, but may be located elsewhere if this is more appropriate. For example, the topic sentence might follow a linking sentence that relates the paragraph to the preceding one.

These features are illustrated in the following paragraph, which is taken from Chapter 1 of this book:

The conceptions of learning and teaching held by teachers and students affect their view of their own role in the learning process. A student who holds the view of learning as knowing more will see the role of the learner and the teacher differently from a student who views learning as understanding the world in new ways. Similarly, a teacher who views teaching as a process of transmission will see the students' role in the learning process differently from a teacher who views teaching as supporting student learning. Therefore, the roles and responsibilities of both students and teachers in the learning process should be clarified.

Its components are as follows:

Topic sentence:

The conceptions of learning and teaching held by teachers and students affect their view of their own role in the learning process.

Supporting sentences:

A student who holds the view of learning as knowing more will see the role of the learner and the teacher differently from a student who views learning as understanding the world in new ways. Similarly, a teacher who views teaching as a process of transmission will see the students' role in the learning process differently from a teacher who views teaching as supporting student learning.

Linking sentence (relating these ideas to the next paragraph):

Therefore, the roles and responsibilities of both students and teachers in the learning process should be clarified.

Teaching paragraph writing

Time required: about 60 minutes

All students will be familiar with writing paragraphs, but some will be more skilful than others. It is important that students become aware of their level of skill before you teach them about paragraph writing, so that they can focus on specific aspects of the process that need attention.

1. Specify a topic that students have covered recently and get them to write a paragraph on the topic. Alternatively, get students to refer to some paragraphs that they have previously written, perhaps for an assignment.
2. Describe the components of an effective paragraph and illustrate them with examples from a textbook or other materials that students are using. Display these components on an overhead or chart. Get students to use

these components to analyse the paragraphs they wrote earlier.

3. Select a topic that students have covered recently and model the process of writing a paragraph on this topic. Refer to the overhead or chart while doing so.
4. Select another topic and ask students to write a paragraph on it. Remind them to avoid whatever weaknesses they had noted in the paragraphs they had written previously.
5. Arrange students in pairs so that they can review each other's paragraphs. Encourage them to refer to the overhead to help them identify the components of these paragraphs.
6. Monitor students' progress and help those who are having difficulty.
7. Invite some students to present their paragraphs to the class for discussion.
8. Ask students to consider the importance of paragraph writing in other courses they are studying, and suggest how they could use paragraph writing in their private study and in study groups.

Using paragraph writing in class activities

Paragraph writing can be used to help students determine how well they understand a topic or idea. Get them to write a paragraph on the topic and then work with a partner to refine it. Tell them to check both for understanding and quality of writing.

At the beginning of a class, get students to write a paragraph describing the most important idea presented in the previous class or in a reading they were set. This will help them make judgements about what is important and also allow them to practise their writing skills. Ask them to read their paragraphs to a small group of peers and explain how they made the decision about what was important.

Other comments

Students can be told to include an in-text reference when they write paragraphs in class. This provides an opportunity for them to practise correct use of in-text referencing. You can then get them to work with a partner to get immediate feedback on their referencing skills.

Paragraph writing can be used to help students evaluate the quality of the notes they make from lectures or their readings. If they use these notes as a basis for writing and referencing a paragraph, it will become obvious whether they are noting enough detail to meet their needs.

Writing summaries from notes

Introduction

Writing a summary from notes is an effective way of increasing students' understanding of the subject matter. It makes them organize the main points they have identified from their lectures and readings, and helps them link ideas together. The process of writing the summary will inform them about their understanding of the content, and give them feedback on the adequacy of their notes.

Description

When students are writing summaries, a major challenge for them is to develop a structure that links together the various ideas used in the summary. Unless they do this their summaries will lack coherence and may be little more than a series of separate points.

When students have made notes from a single lecture or article or chapter from a book, the structure of the summary is likely to be similar to the structure of the original work. However, when they make notes from a variety of sources they will have to develop a new structure for the summary.

Teaching students to write summaries

Time required: about 40 minutes

1. Explain the importance of being able to write effective summaries.
2. Use notes you made from a lecture or reading to demonstrate the process of writing a summary from notes. Pay particular attention to explaining the importance of the structure of the summary.
3. Specify a topic taken from a recent lecture or reading and ask students to write a summary of the topic, using the notes they took at the time.
4. Arrange students into small groups to review their summaries.
5. Ask students individually to determine how adequate their notes were for writing summaries. Get them to plan appropriate action to improve their skills in note making and summarizing.
6. In small groups or on a whole-class basis, have students consider how writing summaries would support their learning in other subjects they are taking. Also get them to consider how they could use the process of writing summaries in their study groups.

Using summaries in class activities

Getting students to write a summary of a lecture they have just attended is an effective way of having them review the lecture. It is also a useful way of reviewing a reading, for it will help them identify the main ideas of the reading and clarify their understanding of these ideas.

Chapter 9:

Strategies for Confirming Learning

The strategies presented in this section are used to help students cope with a variety of assessment situations. In Part One we indicated that assessment can have a powerful effect on student learning, and that assessment tasks should require students to demonstrate their understanding of the material they have learned. Many students have difficulty doing this, and write assignments and answers to examination questions that do little more than reproduce material they have learned. By teaching students how to manage assessment situations, you can make them aware that they have to do more than just reproduce learned material.

In this section we have included strategies that help students work out what is expected of them in the assessment situation, meet those expectations, and learn from feedback they receive.

- Analysing a question and planning a response
- Answering multiple-choice tests
- Assignment preparation
- Learning from feedback
- Preparing for essay examinations

Analysing a question and planning a response

Introduction

Many students have difficulty writing assignments and answering examination questions even though they have a sound knowledge of the subject matter. One reason is that they do not analyse the question properly, or systematically plan a response to it. If they do not analyse the question properly they may overlook an important section, or focus too much attention on minor parts. If they do not plan their answers carefully, they will usually produce work that lacks structure and coherence. If they do not plan their use of time properly, they may find themselves under such pressure to finish an assignment by the due date that they submit an unchecked draft instead of a revised and edited product. In an examination, students who run out of time lose marks for the questions or parts of a question that they have not attempted.

Description

Analysing a question involves using a few simple steps to identify exactly what the question requires. We suggest that students use the following steps:

- circle the verbs that tell them what to do: eg, discuss, compare, analyse
- underline the object of the verb: ie, what they have to discuss or compare or analyse
- identify any other relevant information that affects what they have to do. For example, they might have to answer the question from a particular theoretical perspective
- determine the meaning of the verbs they have circled. To help students do this, we provide them with a list that explains the meaning of the verbs commonly used in our assignment and examination questions. We have included this list at the end of this section. Some verbs have slightly different meanings across different subject areas, so it is important to clarify what is meant by these verbs in your own subject area.

Planning a response to a question involves planning both the content and structure of the response. This involves:

- identifying the specific tasks that have to be completed
- working out the sections that will be used
- listing the main points that will be made
- arranging these points in a logical order.

Another aspect of planning is to ensure that time is used effectively. For information on this, refer to 'Study and time management' in Chapter 10.

Teaching students to analyse a question and plan a response

Time required: about 40 minutes

We suggest that you work with an assignment topic that students will soon have to work on, or an examination question from a previous semester. You will also need another question to use when demonstrating the process. Put this on an overhead transparency.

1. Display the question you have selected for demonstration purposes, and model how to analyse the question and plan a response to it (see 'Modelling learning strategies' in Chapter 11).
2. Get students to read the question that you want them to analyse and
   - Circle the verbs that tell them what to do
   - Underline the object of each verb
   - Identify any other relevant information that affects what they have to do
   - Determine exactly what the verbs mean.
3. Discuss and clarify any questions arising from this activity.
4. Get students individually to identify the main sections that they are likely to include in the assignment.
5. Get them to compare the sections they have identified with those identified by other students.
6. Discuss and clarify these ideas on a whole-class basis.
7. On a whole-class basis, work with students on each of the main sections and list ideas that relate to each section. Get students to plan the reference reading that will be needed to fill any gaps.
8. Discuss with students how useful this process of analysing a question and planning a response to it would be in their other subjects, and how they could use it in study groups.

You may prefer to spread this over two sessions. Work on the first four steps in one class. Direct students to refine their ideas before the next class. In the next class work on the remaining steps.

Using these processes in class activities

Once students are familiar with the skills involved in analysing a question and planning a response to it, you can get them to work with past examination questions, assignment topics and student-generated questions that cover the content you are currently teaching. This will help students identify the important sections of the current topic and determine how well they understand them.

Verbs used in essays

Analyse	identify the component parts of the topic, examine each part in detail and show how the parts relate to each other
Argue	present a case for and/or against a particular proposition. Justify your case by linking it to a particular theory and research evidence
Comment	briefly discuss the topic in a critical way
Compare	present similarities and differences between the items specified
Contrast	present differences between the items specified
Criticize	make judgements about the merit of various features of the particular topic, supporting your judgements with appropriate evidence from theory and research
Define	present the precise meaning of the topic as clearly as possible. Justify any limitations imposed by the definition
Describe	give a detailed account of the topic, using examples to illustrate the various points
Discuss	present in detail all sides of the particular topic, relating them to appropriate evidence from theory and research
Enumerate	present and describe the various items one by one
Evaluate	present an appraisal of the worth of the particular matter in terms of an appropriate frame of reference, such as its usefulness, its truth, or its advantages and disadvantages. Support this by referring to appropriate evidence from theory and research
Examine	describe the particular ideas and comment on their implications
Explain	present the main ideas of the topic in a way that makes their meaning clear to the reader
Identify	list and describe the particular matters
Illustrate	use examples to explain or clarify the topic
Interpret	explain the meaning of the particular matter, on the basis of theory, fact or opinion
Justify	give reasons to support a particular position or conclusion
List	present the information required in a series of notes rather than continuous prose
Outline	present the main features or general principles of the topic in a way that shows how they relate to each other. Do not present minor details
Prove	give sufficient reasons to convince the reader that a position or conclusion is valid
Relate	show how the specified ideas are connected to each other
Review	present a critical survey of the important ideas in the topic. This may involve re-analysing previous conclusions
State	present the required information concisely and clearly

Summarize   present the main ideas or substance of the topic, but do not include details or examples

Trace   present the required ideas in an appropriate chronological order.

Answering multiple-choice tests

Introduction

Many students have difficulty with multiple-choice tests and state that they do not achieve as well in them as they do in other types of tests. One reason for this is that they do not use appropriate strategies to answer the items. For example, some students find it difficult to choose between answers that have similar meanings, while others are reluctant to select a correct answer that seems obvious because they think there might be a trick to the question. Other students develop a false sense of confidence and think that they do not have to study for these tests since they will be able to recognize the correct answer at the time.

Description

There are a number of strategies which students can learn to help them cope better with multiple-choice tests. For example, students should:

- read the instructions and the questions carefully
- actively *think about* each item, and not just read the choices in the hope that they will be able to find the correct answer
- try to generate the correct answer before reading the choices, and then look for it among the alternatives
- delete any answers that are obviously wrong, and then think about the remaining answers to select the best one from those that remain
- use their time effectively and not spend too long on items that are difficult
- choose between answers on the basis of how well they answer the specific question that was asked, not on how correct they are in other contexts
- take a perspective similar to that taken by an expert in the field. This will help them answer questions that do not provide an absolutely correct answer, but require them to select the best choice from those that are offered
- select the more inclusive answer if they are unable to choose between two answers
- examine all the alternatives even if they think they have already found the correct answer
- use information from other questions to help them answer a particular question

- make an informed guess rather than omit an item, unless they know that they stand to lose more marks than they might gain. In the long run, informed guessing usually pays off.

Teaching students to answer multiple-choice tests

Time required: about 30 minutes

The type of question used in multiple-choice tests varies across different subject areas. For example, a multiple-choice test in mathematics is likely to have questions requiring students to select the *correct* answer, whereas a test in sociology might include questions that require students to select the *best* answer. Students should practise with test items in the particular subject areas they study so that they become accustomed to the types of question which are asked in each subject. An effective way of developing students' skill in your particular subject area is to give them test items for practice, and then provide an opportunity for them to discuss how and why they selected particular answers. The following procedure does this:

1. Get students to complete a brief multiple-choice test under examination conditions.
2. Arrange students into small groups to discuss their answers and explain why they chose particular answers. They should also analyse the strategies they used to manage their time in the test.
3. On a whole-class basis, have students discuss and evaluate the strategies they used.
4. Have students consider how useful these strategies would be for answering multiple-choice tests in other subjects they are studying.

Using multiple-choice test items in class activities

Multiple-choice items can be used in class activities to provide feedback to students about their learning and understanding of such material as:

- assigned reading that was done before class
- content presented in a previous class
- ideas just presented in the class.

If you construct a file of items on the various topics you teach, it will be easy to select a few relevant items to use in this way. Computer-based item banks make it very easy to store items and generate short tests.

Get each student to write a couple of multiple-choice items on a topic you have taught. Arrange students into small groups to use the items that they have written to quiz other students. This process helps students revise the subject matter in a detailed way and also gives them practice in answering multiple-choice items.

Caution

Multiple-choice tests often require students only to reproduce knowledge and display a low level of understanding. Having students practise with low level items will give them a false sense of how well they are learning. If you want students to operate at higher cognitive levels, it is important to give them items that require them to *think about* the material.

You will often find multiple-choice items published in work books and test item files that accompany textbooks. These items usually focus on specific subject matter presented in the textbook, and their content may not match the content of the particular course you are teaching. Accordingly, the feedback that students will get by practising with these items may not accurately indicate how well they have learned the subject matter of their own course. Before using items from these sources, you should check them to ensure that they are appropriate to your own course.

Assignment preparation

Introduction

Many problems can arise if students do not use a systematic approach when preparing assignments. For example, if they do not analyse the assignment topic or question properly they may omit an important section or focus on less important parts of the topic. Students who do not properly manage their use of time may not be able to finish the assignment by the due date. They may waste time by taking notes inefficiently or by having to refer back to readings to collect information that they should have noted earlier.

Students who follow a systematic approach to assignment writing are less likely to experience these difficulties. A systematic approach involves analysing the topic, planning the steps involved in writing the assignment, doing the necessary reading, writing the text of the assignment, monitoring progress and checking the end product.

Description

We encourage students to use the following steps:

1. Identify precisely what the assignment requires (see 'Analysing a question and planning a response' earlier in this chapter).
2. Do some initial planning to determine:
   - what content and sections the assignment will contain
   - what information is needed to write these sections
   - a time plan for doing the assignment (see 'Study and time management' in Chapter 10).

3. Do the reference reading and make notes under the sections they have identified (see 'Note making from text' and 'Note making for assignments' in Chapter 7).
4. Check on their progress by reviewing the question and making sure they have addressed all aspects of the question.
5. Draft the introduction. (This is likely to be changed, but it can be helpful for students to draft it before they begin writing the body of the assignment.)
6. Draft the body of the assignment (see 'Writing summaries from notes', 'Organizing ideas' and 'Writing paragraphs' in Chapter 8).
7. Draft the conclusion.
8. Review what they have written, checking for cohesiveness and clarity, and ensuring that they have answered the question and met all the requirements. Revise as required.
9. Edit the revised copy, checking it for technical accuracy.
10. Print the final copy.

Other systematic processes for writing assignments are described in Burdess (1991) and Puhl and Day (1992).

Teaching students how to use a systematic approach to assignment preparation

Time required: about 20 minutes, followed by ongoing practice with component strategies

Most students will already have a particular way of preparing an assignment, and may not heed suggestions that they should use a different approach unless they are convinced that it will work better for them. Therefore, there is little point in trying to teach them about a new method until they indicate some dissatisfaction with their existing method. You can help them determine the effectiveness of their present methods by getting them to reflect on their experience of writing assignments and identify aspects of the process that they could improve.

The following strategy is best taught with reference to an assignment on which students are currently working. This is also the time when students are most likely to be conscious of any weaknesses in the approach that they normally use to prepare assignments.

1. Explain the importance of using a systematic approach to assignment preparation.
2. Explain the steps involved in writing an assignment, and illustrate them by referring to an assignment that students are currently preparing. Details of these steps and advice on how to teach strategies that are used in these steps can be found in the following sections of this book:

Analysing a question and planning a response (earlier in this chapter)
Note making from text, Note making for assignments, and Identifying main points from lectures and readings (Chapter 7)
Writing summaries from notes, Organizing ideas, and Writing paragraphs (Chapter 8)
Study and time management (Chapter 10).

3. Allow students time to discuss these steps in detail, and identify any component strategies that they need to practise.
4. Encourage students to compare this approach with that which they normally use and to consider how useful it would be in other subjects they are studying.

Assessment criteria

The criteria you use for assessing assignments and examinations have a powerful influence on the quality of student learning. If you specify realistic and demanding criteria and advise students of these criteria while they are working on assignments or preparing for examinations, you are likely to produce an improvement in the standard of work and the quality of learning. This will be enhanced if you allow the students to help determine the criteria that will be used to mark their work. We have used the following process to determine criteria for marking an assignment:

1. Get students to analyse the topic and plan a response to it.
2. Arrange students into small groups to consider:
   - the characteristics of an excellent response to the question
   - the characteristics of a response that is just satisfactory
   - how to award the available marks.

   In doing this ask students to consider such matters as the content of the assignment, the use of literature, the level of analysis, and the technical aspects of writing. You should suggest whatever criteria are appropriate to the particular assignment being considered.
3. Get groups to report their suggestions to the whole class. As they do this, build up a set of criteria and guidelines for awarding marks.
4. Use these guidelines as a basis for writing a detailed marking guide, and distribute it to students so they can use it as they prepare the assignment.

We have found that this activity removes much of the uncertainty that is often associated with assignments, without imposing a structure that restricts the way that students can work with the topic. It also increases student awareness of what is important in assignment writing at a time where they can apply this information to improve the quality of their work.

Using these processes in class activities

You can use assignments written in previous semesters to help students improve their assignment writing skills and their understanding of the topic, and to develop an understanding of the standard of work that you expect. Select a number of assignments that range in quality from poor to excellent. Print enough copies for use in your class (you should get students' written permission to copy their assignments, and you must protect their anonymity). Distribute them to students, and get them to work in small groups to:

- analyse the assignment topic
- check whether each assignment meets all the requirements of the question
- note strengths and weaknesses of each assignment.

Explain your opinion of the strengths and weaknesses of the assignments and indicate the grade that you would award to each assignment. This will give students a clearer sense of the standards you expect them to achieve.

You can get students to practise some of the assignment writing skills by working on subject matter from their textbooks. For example, if you want them to practise writing an introduction, you could select a section of the text and ask them to write an introduction to it. Similarly, you could get them to write a conclusion to a particular section of the textbook. These activities require students to read the section, understand its content and work out what is important, and also practise their writing skills.

Learning from feedback

Introduction

Many students do not take advantage of the opportunities they have to learn from the feedback that is provided to them in their course of study. For example, when writing assignments, some students repeat mistakes they made in previous assignments. They do not seem to realize that the feedback given on their previous work is a valuable source of information that can be used to improve subsequent work. Most students do not receive any detailed feedback on their performance in end of semester examinations, and so find it difficult to improve the strategies they use in writing answers to examination questions.

Feedback is not limited to that provided by staff on marked work. Students can provide their own feedback by being reflective and by monitoring the quality of their learning and the learning processes they use. They can also obtain feedback from their peers.

Description

Making effective use of feedback requires students to be reflective about their own work, to heed advice given to them by others, and to be systematic in using this information. The person who marks their work will usually provide an indication of its quality in terms of subject matter, structure and style, and suggest how it could have been improved. Students should identify the specific areas that need attention and plan how they will develop and improve these aspects of their work.

Students will profit from receiving feedback on the processes they use to complete assignments and examinations. For example, they need to know whether their reading strategies are effective, and how efficient they were when they planned the answer to an assignment. They must provide this feedback for themselves, as the person who marks their work can only comment on the finished product and has no knowledge of the processes that were used in producing it. Therefore it is important for students to reflect critically on the processes they use in preparing assignments and writing examinations. Most students will need a considerable amount of guidance and encouragement to do this, for they usually have depended on the teacher to give them feedback.

Feedback can also be obtained from peers in class activities. Many of the activities suggested in this book involve peer interaction, which provides an opportunity for students to receive feedback on their learning and understanding, as well as on their thinking and working processes. It is necessary to alert students explicitly to this source of feedback, since many of them will not be accustomed to receiving feedback from peers.

Teaching students to make effective use of feedback

Feedback from assignments

Time required: two sessions, each about 25 minutes

It is important to encourage students to be reflective about what they have learned from doing an assignment, in terms of both the subject matter and the processes they used to prepare the assignment. The following activity will help students reflect on the processes they use for assignment preparation. An appropriate time for this activity is when students have submitted their first assignment.

1. Explain to students the importance of using feedback for self-improvement.
2. Remind students of the various activities that they should have used when preparing the assignment, and ask them to reflect on how well they performed each of these activities. They might consider how they analysed the question, planned the response to it, used their time, made notes, gathered information, and wrote and edited their work.
3. Ask them to list a couple of features of the assignment that they are really pleased with, and a couple of features that they are less pleased with.
4. Get them to share their reflections and lists with a partner and discuss the strategies and processes they found to be effective. They should also discuss how they could have handled any problems they experienced.

5. Have students plan to avoid difficulties when they prepare their next assignment. They might write a reminder to themselves in their diaries, or annotate the course outline where the details of the next assignment are presented.

We have also found it useful to get students to attach to their assignments a self-reflective statement that focuses on the processes they used in preparing the assignment. We ask them to write about 300 words on the following:

- what they did when they were preparing the assignment that helped their learning and understanding, and explain how it helped
- what they would do differently to enhance their learning and understanding if they were doing an assignment like this again, and why they would do it differently
- what they learned about the subject matter and the assignment writing process from doing this assignment.

This provides a record of their learning processes that they can refer to later to improve the quality of their assignment work.

After you return marked assignments to the students, you can focus student attention on the quality of their assignments. It is often best to wait a few days before doing this, because students will need time to read the assignment and reflect on the marker's comments. Some students also need time to work through feelings of disappointment about the mark that they received. About a week after the assignments have been returned, you could do the following:

1. Get students to review their assignments and the marker's comments prior to coming to class, and to note some targets for improvement. They should try to identify at least one aspect of the subject matter which needs further work and one matter relating to the structure or style of the assignment.
2. In class, review the question and discuss how it should have been answered. Pay attention to structure and style as well as content.
3. Get students to share their assignments so that they all read at least one assignment which received a higher mark than their own or which has a particularly strong feature.
4. Get them to identify features in that assignment that contributed to higher marks. This will involve the content of the assignment as well as its structure and style.
5. Tell students to relate these features to the specific targets for improvement that they developed from reflecting on their own assignment.
6. Advise students to make an entry in their diaries or an annotation on the requirements for the next assignment that describes what they plan to do to improve the quality of their next assignment.

Feedback from examinations

Time required: no specific requirement, for this is treated incidentally

Feedback from examinations can provide information about the processes that students used in the examination and about the quality of their learning. Students will have to generate their own feedback about the processes they used in the examination situation, such as analysing questions, planning answers and monitoring their use of time. You can encourage them to do this by suggesting that they spend a few minutes after each examination reflecting on what went well and what they could have done to perform better. They should make a note of these matters and try to apply them in their next examinations.

Giving students feedback on their performance in the examination is difficult to arrange, particularly for end of semester and end of year examinations. Once they have finished a course, most students are not interested in finding out details of their examination performance, apart from knowing the marks they obtained. In particular, few students are interested in working on gaps in their learning after they have completed a course. However, if you are committed to helping students improve their learning and performance, you should encourage them to consult with their lecturers after the examination, look at their examination scripts and note what they could do to improve their preparation and performance.

Preparing for essay examinations

Introduction

Writing answers to essay questions in an examination requires the same processes and skills that are used in other types of writing. These include:

- knowledge and understanding of the subject matter
- skill in planning the structure of an essay
- skill in expressing one's ideas.

However, writing in examinations places additional demands on writers, since they usually have to work within strict time limits with little or no access to resources. They also have no opportunity to revise a draft answer, and have to submit the work in their own handwriting. Therefore it is useful for students to be familiar with the special requirements of writing in examinations and to have spent some time practising this type of writing.

Description

In the examination situation students have to:

- analyse the question to determine what is being asked of them
- plan the structure of the answer
- identify the content to be included in each section of the answer
- write the answer
- review the answer.

We have explained the skills of analysing a question and planning an answer in the section 'Analysing a question and planning a response', earlier in this chapter. In this section we address the remaining tasks.

Teaching students how to answer essay questions in examinations

Time required: two sessions, one about 40 minutes, the other about 30 minutes

Even though most students have heard advice about the importance of planning and managing their time in examinations, many of them do not heed it in stressful examination situations. The following procedure will make them more aware of the importance of planning, and give them practice in doing this:

1. Give students an examination question relating to work that has been covered recently. Tell them that they have ten minutes to work with it in the same way they would use the first ten minutes of an examination.
2. Arrange the students into small groups to discuss what they did during the ten minutes, and to identify the steps they followed. The intention is for them to identify appropriate ways of using the time to plan an answer to the question.
3. Obtain feedback from the groups on appropriate ways to plan an answer.
4. Get the groups to consider possible ways of structuring the answer to this particular question.
5. Tell students to refine their planned answers and write a full answer to the question in their own time under examination conditions and bring it to the next class.
6. In the next class, arrange students into pairs and get them to compare their answers, both in terms of content and structure.
7. Select some answers to read to the whole class for comment.
8. Get students to consider how they could use this process in other courses they are studying, in their private study and with study groups.

Another way to teach this
If you have access to students' examination papers from a previous semester,

---

you can use them to help students get a sense of the standards expected of them. Select a question that relates to subject matter that has been covered recently, and locate three answers: a poor answer, an average one and a good one. Make sufficient copies for each person in the class, making sure that you protect the writer's anonymity.

1. Distribute or display the question and get students individually to analyse it and to plan an answer.
2. Distribute the three answers you have copied and get students to note strengths and weaknesses of each, and to rank the answers in order or award each a grade.
3. Arrange students in pairs or small groups to compare their evaluations.
4. Conduct a whole-class discussion on the features of the three answers, covering both their content and structure.
5. Explain the rank or grade that you would have awarded to each answer, and discuss any significant differences between the students' assessments and your own.

Using examination questions in class activities

Select an examination question that relates to work covered in a recent class. Get them to plan an answer to it and list the content that they would include in the answer. This gets students to revise the subject matter as well as giving them practice in planning an answer.

Select an examination question that relates to reading that students were expected to do before a class. Get them to plan an answer to it and to list the content they would include in the answer. This might encourage students to do the preliminary reading that is set for future classes.

Caution

Do not place too much emphasis on writing for examination purposes, because students might conclude that preparation for the examination is the most important focus of learning.

Chapter 10:

Personal Management Strategies

Only two strategies are presented in this section. Neither of them is directly focused on learning, but students who understand them and use them well are likely to find that they have a positive effect on the quality of their learning. Many students are busy with activities outside the university, such as family, social, recreational and employment commitments. Effective time management can help them cope with these conflicting demands. Some students find that the student role is more complex than they expected, and to cope with this role they have to learn about many aspects of the university situation.

- Coping with the student role
- Study and time management

Coping with the student role

Introduction

Many students have difficulty coping with the complexity of the university environment. It is often quite different from their previous experience. It usually provides them with less support than they received at school since they are expected to be responsible for their own behaviour. Some beginning students become anxious because they are not clear about what will happen during the semester and they do not know how well they will cope with difficulties. This anxiety will affect the quality of their learning.

Description

As a university teacher you are an important contact person for the student. Even though you may not be directly involved in the problems that students face, you should be able to give them advice or tell them where they can get good advice. Some situations with which students have to cope and which can cause anxiety include:

- course selection and enrolment procedures
- finding out the role of the academic skills adviser or student counsellor and contacting them
- how to access the computer laboratories
- how to use the library or audio-visual centre
- how to make up work they missed because of sickness or other absence from class
- what to do if they feel they have been unfairly assessed in an assignment or examination
- procedures for submitting assignments
- what to do if they cannot submit an assignment by the due date
- what to do if they miss a test or examination
- role of the student union
- how the provisional examination timetable works.

Helping students meet these challenges

Some institutions provide an orientation period in which students can learn about their new role. However, students cannot anticipate all their needs, especially when they are in a new environment. Nor are they likely to understand and remember information about a new situation that is presented outside a context of personal need. We believe that it is better to provide students with this information closer to the point of need when it will be seen as something that is important for them to know about.

Not all student concerns will relate to the course you teach. However, we believe that it is still important for you to give students an opportunity to raise their concerns, for even if they are not directly related to your course, they are likely to affect student performance in it. You can anticipate some student concerns and arrange for them to be raised at an appropriate time in the semester. For example, early in the semester you can discuss what students should do if they become sick and miss classes. When they are working on the first assignment you should advise them how to ask for an extension of time if they cannot complete the assignment by the due date. Towards the end of the semester you should remind them of examination policies and procedures.

Caution

Keep in mind that you should encourage students to accept responsibility for their own behaviour and not become dependent on lecturers and other staff. While it is appropriate to provide students with information, it is not helpful to solve their problems for them. It is better to advise students about the procedures to be followed in a particular situation and require them to follow these procedures for themselves.

Study and time management

Introduction

Most students have many demands made on their time, such as the demands of study, employment, family commitments, social activities and recreation. It is important for students to manage their time well so that they can cope with these demands. This will involve them in reflecting on their priorities and scheduling enough time to allow them to meet these priorities.

Description

Key elements of effective time management include long-term planning such as planning over a full semester, medium-term planning covering the forthcoming week, and short-term planning for the next day.

Effective planning at any of these levels involves developing a schedule that caters for all the demands that compete for a student's time. A schedule does not have to be very detailed. At first it might only cover broad areas, leaving details to be filled in closer to the time of implementation.

Long-term planning
One way of developing a long-term schedule is the following:

1. Obtain a semester planner that provides a box for each day of the semester.
2. Enter all the givens associated with study, such as when examinations will be held and when assignments are due.
3. Enter other important details, such as employment commitments, recreational activities or family matters.
4. Working backwards from the deadlines, decide when particular tasks will be attended to: for example doing the reading for an assignment, or revising for examinations.

Once a long-term plan of this type has been developed, students can see when their major commitments are due, when their busy periods are, and when they have time to devote to other activities. They can then schedule these activities at an appropriate time.

We do not believe that there is only one way to develop a schedule, and we encourage students to experiment with different forms and adopt one that works well for them.

Medium-term planning

When students have completed this level of planning they can plan for the forthcoming week on a more detailed basis. They will need to prepare a timetable that covers the full week. A diary is suitable for this purpose. In this they enter details of any fixed commitments for the week, such as classes that they have to attend, and employment and social activities. Then they can schedule the other things they plan on doing in that week, such as preparation for class, reviewing after class, preparation of assignments and study for examinations.

Short-term planning

The most detailed level of planning is the daily plan which involves fine tuning of the weekly plan. It provides a detailed plan of the day's activities and often focuses on a single task.

Another aspect of effective study management is for students to ensure that they make best use of the time they have scheduled for particular activities. They could be encouraged to:

- set realistic time limits for completing particular tasks
- schedule the most challenging tasks at the time when they find it easiest to work
- assign blocks of time to complex tasks and keep short periods of time for simple or more fragmented tasks
- always have some work with them that they can do if they find themselves with some free time, such as when they are waiting at a bus stop or waiting for an appointment, or when a class is cancelled
- carry a notebook in which they can write ideas and thoughts about their studies.

Teaching students to make effective use of time

Time required: about 35 minutes

1. Discuss the importance of effective study and time management.
2. Ask a few students to describe how they manage their study time and to indicate how effectively this works.
3. Explain how students can plan on a long-, medium- and short-term basis in order to use their time efficiently and effectively.
4. Get students to draw up a long-term schedule and then a schedule for the forthcoming week. Give them some advice on how long it might take them to complete activities such as reading for an assignment or writing the assignment.
5. Get students to work in small groups to compare their schedules and to share ideas they have for using time effectively. In doing this it may be useful to group students according to their personal roles: eg, young students living at home, part-time students, parents with young children. Common interests make it easier for them to help each other to schedule their time effectively.

Caution

You should encourage students to see planning as an ongoing process which produces schedules that are subject to change. Otherwise, students are likely to stop using time plans if they have difficulty keeping to them. Students should develop schedules with the expectation that they may have to refine them as circumstances change.

Chapter 11:

Teaching Strategies

This section is provided to draw attention to some challenges that will arise when you teach learning strategies. For example, since we place considerable importance on cooperative small group learning, we thought it would be useful to give some advice on teaching small groups. The jigsaw method describes a particular way of working with groups that helps students learn with understanding. We believe that when you introduce an innovation it is important to clarify your expectations with students and get regular feedback from them on their reactions to the innovation, so we have outlined ways of doing this.

- Clarifying expectations with students
- Getting feedback from students
- Modelling learning strategies
- Teaching small groups
- The jigsaw method

Clarifying expectations with students

Introduction

Students will come to your classes holding certain conceptions of learning and teaching: expectations about how they will go about learning and how you will go about teaching. Similarly, you will have expectations of the students: how they will approach their learning and participate in class activities. Any significant mismatch between your expectations and theirs is likely to reduce the effectiveness of your teaching and the quality of their learning. Therefore it is important to clarify your expectations to the students and give them an opportunity to communicate their expectations to you. This is especially important when you introduce an innovative programme that involves a significant change to the usual ways of teaching or learning.

Description

Although this can be done individually, we have found it better to work on a small group basis in a way that protects the anonymity of students who make suggestions. One way of doing this is as follows:

1. Get students to reflect individually on what they expect of you as the teacher and how they expect the classes to be conducted.
2. Arrange students into small groups to share their expectations and to develop a list of expectations that are acceptable to all members of the group.
3. Get each group to report these expectations to the whole class. Encourage discussion among students about the various matters raised. Whenever appropriate, respond to their expectations by telling the students your expectations of them. If you cannot agree to a particular matter they raise, explain why you cannot agree and work with students to resolve the matter.
4. Note the expectations that students report, and later in the semester collect feedback from students about how well they were met.

Getting feedback from students

Introduction

Most university staff are accustomed to getting feedback from students at the end of a semester, and many universities have established formal procedures for doing this. This feedback can give staff useful information about the courses they teach and can help them improve these courses. We believe that it is also important to get feedback from students early in the semester so that you can monitor student progress and make adjustments to the course before problems arise. Getting feedback on a regular basis gives students an opportunity to influence the nature of the course and the way they respond to it. This is likely to enhance their commitment to the course and improve the quality of their learning.

Description

It is not necessary to restrict yourself to formal processes when obtaining feedback from students. One simple approach that we use involves giving students a sheet of paper and asking them to write for five minutes on any aspect of the course that comes to mind. This is an easy way of finding out how students perceive the course. If you do this early in the semester, you can address any concerns that students have and adjust the course so that students can participate more effectively in it.

It is important for you to share this feedback with the students. Tell them about the positive features they noted, and indicate how you will address the concerns they raised.

Sometimes it will be better to adopt a more structured procedure. We have found it useful to use a small group approach that protects the anonymity of students and is relatively non-threatening to them. One way of doing this is as follows:

1. Get students individually to reflect on the course or on specific aspects of it, and make notes about their perceptions.
2. Arrange students into small groups to share their perceptions and determine which perceptions are held by several members of the group.
3. Get each group to report these perceptions to the whole class. If students are uncomfortable about reporting their perceptions in class, get each group to submit their reports in writing.
4. Where problems are identified, discuss them with students in order to find a solution. You may do this immediately, or you may wish to wait for a few days so that you can consider appropriate ways of responding to the problem.
5. Later in the semester collect feedback from students about how well these problems were solved.

Modelling learning strategies

Introduction

When teaching students a learning strategy, you should expect them to acquire three types of knowledge: knowledge about the strategy (declarative knowledge), knowledge of how to use it (procedural knowledge) and knowledge about when and why to use it (conditional knowledge). Therefore as well as telling students about the strategy, you should show them how, when and why to use it. An effective way of doing this is to model the use of the strategy.

Description

Modelling involves demonstrating how to do something. However, whereas a demonstration usually shows how an expert performs the process in a way that is free from hesitation and errors, modelling includes showing the decision-making components that help the expert decide which process should be used and how to use it.

In teaching learning strategies, 'think-aloud modelling' is often used. In this type of modelling, instead of just showing students how to use the strategy, the teacher verbalizes and demonstrates what she or he thinks about when using the strategy. In addition to providing *procedural knowledge* about how to implement the strategy, this process provides *conditional knowledge* about how the decision to use the particular strategy is made, how progress is monitored, how difficulties are handled, and so on. In other words, think-aloud modelling makes explicit the metacognitive aspects of strategy use.

Think-aloud modelling can be used to demonstrate most of the learning strategies described in this book. When using the process, it is important to model the uncertainties and difficulties that students are likely to experience so that attention is drawn to the metacognitive aspects of using the strategy.

Teaching small groups

Introduction

Small group teaching is one of the most demanding forms of university teaching. It involves transferring some of the control of what happens in the class to the students, whose individual differences, interests, knowledge of the subject matter and willingness to get involved with it will affect the course of the lesson. When you work with small groups there will always be some uncertainty about the exact direction the class will follow and the outcomes of the session.

Description

Successful group management involves careful planning before the class as well as close attention to the management of group processes during the class.

Planning
Some specific matters that should be considered include the following:

- How will the groups be formed? Sometimes it is sufficient to let students decide their own groups, but at other times you will want to impose some structure on the groups.
- What size groups will you use? You should be prepared to vary the size of sub-groups according to the activities you have planned. Working in pairs is useful where you want students to check each other's understanding of key ideas, while working in threes provides an opportunity for the third person to act as an observer and report on the processes that

were used by the other two. If groups consist of more than about five people their effectiveness is usually reduced, since there are fewer opportunities for interaction and it becomes easier for individuals not to participate in group activities.

- How will the furniture be arranged? When students are working in groups, everyone in the group should be able to make eye contact with everyone else. In order to make this possible, it may be necessary to rearrange the furniture in some way. It is well worth spending whatever time is needed to do this.
- How much time will you allocate to each activity? It is just as important to plan the use of time in a small group activity as it is in other forms of teaching.

Management of group processes

In order for small groups to operate effectively, it is important that you:

- provide students with an overview of the session. It is good practice to let students know how the class time will be used. This gives them a clearer sense of the purpose of the various activities and how they relate to each other
- explain the purpose of each activity. Group activities often seem to lack a clear purpose, and can drift into aimless conversations. Making the purpose of an activity explicit will help to keep students focused, and will also help you judge how effective the activity is for student learning
- provide clear instructions. Be quite explicit with your instructions to groups, and be prepared to question students to ensure that they have understood the instructions. Write instructions on a whiteboard or an overhead transparency and leave them visible while students are engaged in the task
- establish time limits for each activity. Tell students how long they have for each activity, and monitor their progress. Adjust the time allocation as necessary
- get students to plan what notes they intend to make during the activity. Many students treat group activities as occasions where it is unnecessary to take notes, and they finish with no permanent record of what happened in the group. Group activities can provide important ideas, and many of them are likely to be forgotten unless students make a note of them
- at the end of a group activity, provide an opportunity for students to consolidate their learning. This might involve them in writing a paragraph summarizing what they have learned, or explaining to a partner what they have learned
- where possible, you should participate in the group activities. This will give you feedback on how well the activities work, and how well students

understand the course material. However, do not allow yourself to become too involved in the work of a particular group, and take care that students do not rely on you to act as the group leader or be the subject matter expert.

The jigsaw method

Introduction

The jigsaw method is so called because each student works on only one part of a learning task and then works with other students to combine the various parts and complete the task. It is an effective method of learning because it requires students to work on a section of the topic with the intention of being able to explain it to others. The process of explaining to others has a powerful effect on the quality of learning achieved by the explainer (Dansereau, 1988).

Description

The jigsaw method is most easily used when the learning task can be divided into a number of discrete sections, each of which can be learned independently of the others. It involves giving each student one section of the task to study and explain to other students, as described below:

1. Assign each student one of the sections and an appropriate reading and get them to summarize the main ideas presented in that section.
2. Arrange students into small groups, with each group comprising students who have focused on the same section. If there are three sections to the task, there will be three different types of group.
3. In these groups, have students check their understanding of the section with other students who have studied the same material.
4. Rearrange students into groups covering all the sections of the task. Each group will contain one student who studied the first section, another who studied the second section, and so on.
5. Get students to take turns explaining their section of the task to the others in the group.
6. Conclude the activity by reviewing important ideas and attending to any questions that arose in the small groups.

The jigsaw approach avoids one problem that is often encountered in small groups: students working from a position of ignorance. The initial activity of having students study a specific section of the task informs them about their particular section, so that in the final activity each group consists of informed discussants.

We illustrated the jigsaw method by referring to students learning new material from reading done in class. Although readings are commonly used, they are not essential. For example, you might want students to examine an issue from a number of theoretical perspectives. If you use a jigsaw approach for this activity, you might assign each student a particular theoretical perspective to use in examining the issue. Each student would have to think about the issue from the assigned perspective, and then explain it to peers who had used a different perspective.

Part 3: Teaching learning strategies in context

Chapter 12:

A Programme for University Teachers

Background

We had been involved in researching student learning and teaching students learning strategies for a number of years. We had demonstrated that students could be taught learning strategies and that their knowledge and understanding of subject matter improved. However, even though we had shown that learning strategies could be taught at the same time as subject matter, and that it was effective in improving student learning, only our own students were being taught in this way. If teaching students learning strategies is good practice, and if the learning strategies and teaching methods we use are theoretically sound and practical, as we believe they are, then other university teachers should be able to teach them. Our university agreed, and provided us with support to develop and implement a programme where university teachers would learn to teach learning strategies to their students.

We were aware that setting up a programme to prepare teachers to implement an innovation is not easy. Educational innovations involving changes in curriculum or teaching methods may be effective in pilots or trials, but often fail to achieve the same results when applied by others across wider educational contexts. We believed that if our programme were to be successful, we would have to select teachers who were strongly motivated to help their students learn. In conducting this programme, we would have to foster the development of well-structured knowledge of the principles of learning and strategy instruction. This would require us to conduct the sessions in a way that encouraged active learning by each participant, and interaction between all participants.

Selection of teachers to participate in the programme

We identified specific criteria for selecting teachers to participate in the programme. We wanted:

- teachers who were willing to devote the time and effort that would be needed to develop and implement a programme
- experienced and competent teachers who were confident in teaching subject matter
- teachers who were concerned about their students' learning
- to work with teachers from a variety of disciplines, because their varied experience and background would enrich our programme and confirm that learning strategies can be taught by university teachers from a variety of subject areas
- to include more than one teacher from each of the particular disciplines, so that they could support each other, and provide applications and ideas of the concepts and strategies covered in the programme.

We informed all teaching staff throughout the university of the purpose and structure of the programme and invited them to attend an information session at which we provided more details. We then asked the teachers who were still interested in participating to complete a form indicating their reasons for wanting to be involved in the programme and the course in which they intended to implement their own programme. On the basis of our selection criteria we invited 14 teachers to participate. These teachers were considered by their peers to be good teachers, and many had received Teaching Excellence Awards. Since the selection had been competitive, with many more applications than places available, there was a sense that the selected teachers had won a place in the programme, rather than just having been selected into it. As a consequence they were positive and committed at the outset.

Structure and content of the programme

The programme took place over six days. Two weeks before the start of semester, participants attended for three consecutive days. One week later they attended for one day. They then attended for another day during the mid-semester break, and for the final day early in the examination week at the end of semester.

Day 1: Introduction to the concepts and theory

The purpose of Day 1 was to provide a common purpose and language for the rest of the programme. Participants were introduced to the central concepts and theory presented in Part One of this book. They were asked to identify the purpose of university education from their own perspective and to consider their conceptions of teaching and learning. They then worked through a series of activities that illustrated the learning process and introduced a range of learning strategies. In this way they were involved in a variety of group and individual tasks that introduced the concepts on which the programme was based. In addition, each person was given a draft copy of this book and encouraged to read Part One to clarify their understanding of the concepts.

Day 2: Detailed introduction to learning strategies

The purpose of Day 2 was to introduce the participants to the full range of learning strategies so they could select the strategies appropriate for their course. Two strategies were taught and modelled to demonstrate the process of strategy instruction and modelling thinking. The learning processes that were involved in teaching and using each strategy were emphasized. The content of the activities was drawn from the content of Part One of this book to illustrate how the learning strategies could be taught at the same time as the subject matter.

Day 3: Clarifying the task and developing the programme

The purpose of Day 3 was to provide participants with the opportunity to reconsider their teaching, their subject matter and their goals. This was important because teachers rarely reconsider courses and programmes that are familiar to them, particularly when they are under pressure at the beginning of a semester.

First, participants identified the goals they wanted their students to achieve as a result of studying their course. Each person then analysed their course and the constraints associated with the teaching context, the students, and the students' approaches to learning. On the basis of their analysis of their course and the goals they wanted to achieve, they planned the semester programme of subject matter and learning strategies for their course.

Participants identified a number of issues they wanted to cover in the remainder of the programme. They included assessment, overseas students studying in Australia, and developing self-directed learning materials. These issues were addressed in the subsequent days of the programme.

Day 4: Review of planning

The purpose of Day 4 was to provide the opportunity for participants to review their plans and programmes and to practise teaching a selected learning strategy. Participants presented their programmes to the others in a small group. They outlined their purpose and identified the learning strategies and subject matter they were intending to teach. They then taught one of their selected strategies to a small group. The purpose of this was to get each person to practise teaching a learning strategy to a supportive audience, and to receive comments on their teaching. The participants were very active in contributing suggestions and comments and asking for clarification. In this way they encouraged each other to articulate their goals and intentions, and provided valuable comments and suggestions for implementing their programmes.

Day 5: Monitoring the programmes

The purpose of Day 5 was to provide an opportunity for reflection, review and encouragement to continue with the programme. The participants were asked to report on their programmes in terms of their successes and difficulties, and their students' and their own reactions to the programme. They were also asked to present a learning strategy they had successfully taught during their programme. Again the participants sought clarification, probed, encouraged and offered suggestions to each other. If someone had found that a particular activity or strategy had not worked, they sought reasons for this and considered suggestions and advice. Many went away with new ideas to try, fresh ways of approaching a task, and encouragement to keep on with their programmes.

Day 6: Review of programmes and outcomes

The purpose of Day 6 was to get participants to review and reflect on their own programmes, to consider how they might overcome difficulties, and build on successes in their future teaching. The participants reported to the whole group on their programmes in terms of successes and difficulties, their students' and their own reactions. They concluded by indicating what changes and adjustments they felt should be made and what they intended doing in the future.

Case studies

Participants were asked to develop a case study of their programme. This would provide details of their intentions in conducting the programme, the strategies they taught, and the outcomes they achieved. In the next chapter we present a selection of these case studies.

Chapter 13:

Case Studies

The participants in the staff development programme were asked to prepare a case study on the development of, and their reflections on, their programmes. These case studies were compiled over the six days of the programme. At the end of each day the participants were asked to work on their case studies, and these formed the basis of their presentations on subsequent days. The case study was an important part of the programme as it required participants to plan, record, report and reflect on their teaching programmes over the whole semester. It required them to record not only what they did, but how it worked, and why it was or was not successful. It also required them to reflect on possible changes and the further implementation of their programme.

A selection of edited case studies from different subject areas is presented in this chapter.

- Science
- Language studies
- Early childhood education
- Accounting
- Information science

Science

Contributed by Monica Leggett, Department of Applied Science

The teacher

Monica has taught and researched at Edith Cowan University for seven years. Before that, she was a lecturer at Curtin University of Technology. She has also taught in secondary schools and worked in the power industry. Her main teaching interests are in the area of scientific and technological literacy, and she focuses on teaching for understanding and empowerment. Her research interests are centred on public perceptions of technology.

The course

Monica taught in the second year course 'Technology in Society', which is part of the Bachelor of Applied Science (Technology Studies). This course examines the origins and nature of technology and its relation with science and society. Most students who took the course also took supporting studies in business, environmental management, science or computing. An important objective of the course was to challenge students' assumptions and beliefs about the connections between technology and society by looking at past developments and current issues. Another objective was to develop students' understanding of the complexity of interactions between science, technology and society.

Students attended classes for four hours each week during the 13-week semester. These classes involved both lectures and tutorials. Students were encouraged to participate in a programme of visits to organizations and centres where they could experience the use of old and new technology. The course included three formal assessments: a group tutorial presentation, a written essay assignment and an end of semester examination.

The students

Most of the students in this course came to university directly from secondary schools, but there were also a few mature and overseas students. Most students took the course as part of their major area of study, with a smaller number taking it as a minor area of study. Many of the students did not have a clearly defined career path.

Many of the students taking the course seemed to want to do only the minimum amount of work needed to achieve a pass. The majority of them were accustomed to focusing on memorizing and reproducing information covered in courses rather than understanding it. There has been a degree of tension between the students who aimed to understand and those who wanted to complete the course with least effort.

The purpose of the learning strategies programme

Monica had identified two main problems that she wanted to address. One problem related to the low level of understanding and engagement with the subject that was evident in previous students' tutorial and essay assignments. The other problem related to the difficulty of getting students to integrate prior knowledge with new information. Students seemed to make little attempt to confront conflicting ideas, acknowledge value judgements, and challenge them critically.

Monica hoped to address these problems by focusing on how students acquired and worked with information and how she assessed their learning. She decided to teach students about the following learning strategies: study and time management, identifying main points from lectures and readings, note making from text, writing summaries from notes, note making from lectures, organizing ideas, generating questions, assignment preparation, preparing for essay examinations and making concept maps. In addition, she adjusted the scope and criteria of the tutorial presentation and essay assignment to encourage students to work with the material and develop better understanding of the subject matter.

Monica integrated the teaching of these strategies with the subject matter of the course by introducing the strategies as they were required by the students. For example, she presented note making from text as a way of introducing students to a central reading required for tutorials and assessment activities. Then she taught students how to write a summary based on their notes. In this way students learned about note making and summary writing as they carried out the reading that was needed for their class work and their assignment.

Another example of the integration of learning strategies with subject matter is seen when students were taught to generate questions to help them work with information. This strategy was first taught with lecture material that students had previously found challenging. It was later practised in the context of helping students revise for the examination by generating questions and writing summaries of important topics.

Monica also involved the students in negotiating the criteria for assessing the tutorial presentation and essay assignment, and in setting up groups to organize and present the tutorials.

Reactions to the learning strategies programme

Successes
Monica felt that she achieved a number of small successes. At the end of the course the students seemed better prepared to handle their third-year studies in science, both in terms of their understanding of the subject matter and their

use of learning strategies. The tutorial presentation assignment was success-ful, and students worked better in groups and presented work that addressed the relationships between technology and society more thoroughly than had occurred in previous years. The tutorials featured more group discussion and the presentations were more informative and interesting for the audience.

The students initially responded to the programme with inertia and some complacency. They felt that they had heard it all before at school and did not need to work on their learning strategies. However, this attitude changed as the semester progressed, and they became more willing to learn about the strategies and to try to use them. By the end of semester Monica felt that the programme had raised students' awareness of learning strategies and study techniques and had convinced them that their use of these strategies could be made more effective.

At the end of semester, feedback from students indicated that they were quite positive about the introduction of learning strategies into the course. When they were asked to indicate the three most important things they had learned in the course, many students mentioned not only subject matter knowledge and understanding but learning strategies as well. For example, one student reported that the three most important things she learned were, 'better study techniques, the three waves of technology, and the societal changes that occur with changing technology'. Another student commented that 'the study skills were good and gave me a better idea of what I should be doing'.

One of the most important outcomes for Monica was that she became more aware of the extent to which students do not know or use techniques that she had expected them to know and use in the course. She also felt that the programme stimulated her to reconsider her own conception of teaching and her priorities as a teacher.

Difficulties

The main difficulty that Monica experienced in the programme related to time: identifying how much time was needed to teach the various strategies, and allocating enough time to teach them properly. She was surprised at how long it took to teach the strategies, and found that she could not keep to her original schedule. Part way through the semester she reviewed the pro-gramme with the students and decided not to teach all the strategies that she had intended. Instead, she focused on reviewing and practising the strategies that she had already taught.

Early in the semester Monica felt that she was spending too much time on the learning strategies and not enough time covering the subject matter. At first she was hesitant and almost apologetic in teaching the strategies, for she expected that most students would have covered them at school. Later, as she became more aware of students' needs and saw that the integration of strategies and subject matter was working, she became more confident about her approach.

Monica experienced particular difficulties when teaching students to make notes from text. She had not realized how little some students gain from their reading or how long it took them to read. Nor had she realized how many of them could not read flexibly, and she underestimated how different it was for them to read and make notes in the recommended way. She now realizes that she should make reading easier for students by selecting different reading materials and by providing more guidance and practice in how to identify the main ideas in a reading and make notes from it.

Students were reluctant to participate in negotiating the criteria for presenting and assessing assignments, and simply accepted her suggestions about the criteria that would be used and the marks that would be assigned. Despite this, Monica felt that the students obtained a better understanding of the criteria.

Early in the semester, most students resisted being taught learning strategies. This was particularly evident in the attitude of the younger students. Although their resistance declined as the semester progressed, it did cause some difficulties and required extra effort on Monica's part to get the students to accept the programme.

Future directions

Having tried the techniques, Monica now feels a greater sense of confidence and ownership of the programme. She believes this confidence will allow her more freedom to adapt the techniques to fit the context and allow for better integration of the strategies and the content.

She intends to review the content of the course before she next teaches it. In doing this she will consider the learning strategies that are needed in the course as well as its subject matter.

Monica recognizes that it is difficult for teachers to resist students' expectations that they should present factual content and information for students to learn and reproduce. However, she believes that if teachers integrate the learning strategies with the subject matter and help students work with information to develop understanding, it becomes easier to resist these expectations.

Reflections

Monica felt that having the opportunity to develop her programme as part of a group of other teachers helped her learn about strategies and how to teach them. It enabled her to talk over difficulties and find solutions from other teachers' experiences. It also stimulated her to reflect on her own practice and beliefs about teaching and learning.

My own attitude to the process has changed. Initially I was hesitant, almost apologetic in my teaching of the strategies, knowing that most of my students had covered them at school. However, my discovery of the real need, together with informal conversations with students about the strategies which they have been taught to use at school, changed this.

Language studies

Contributed by Graham McKay, Department of Language Studies

The teacher

Graham has taught and researched at Edith Cowan University for ten years. Before that, he taught at the Darwin Institute of Technology School of Australian Linguistics. He also worked as a linguist with the Australian Department of Education. His main teaching interests are in the area of linguistics. His research interests are centred around descriptive linguistics, the Aboriginal languages of Arnhem Land, and vernacular literacy in indigenous languages.

The course

Graham taught the first year course 'Introduction to language studies', which is an introductory course for a number of Bachelor of Arts programmes. These programmes include major studies in the various languages, minor studies in linguistics, and the secondary education English course. The course provided a basic introduction to language and linguistics to students from a variety of language backgrounds. It focused on providing an overview of the concepts and terminology of linguistics in terms of the social, cultural, structural and communicative aspects of language. These include language variation, language and context, language structures and language learning.

Students attended one three-hour class each week over the 13-week semester. The classes were arranged in a way that allowed for lectures, group discussions and other interactive activities. Students completed three formal assessments: two sets of worksheet assignments and an examination. The worksheets covered the course work from the previous weeks; for example, Assignment 1 covered the topics from the first five weeks. Students could hand in their worksheets progressively each week or submit them all on the due date.

The students

The students in this course varied greatly. About half of them spoke a second language, with some speaking up to three or four languages. These included languages from Asia, Africa and Europe. Students who spoke a second language may have had some basic knowledge of linguistics terminology and concepts, but others had very little awareness of basic terminology or tools of analysis.

Many students aimed just to pass the course because it was a prescribed part of their programme. A number of students resisted challenges to their present understanding of language. On the other hand, some students were highly interested in language and languages and wanted to explore and learn as much as they could. Many students had a limited perception of the relevance of linguistics to their field of study, and focused their learning just on meeting assessment requirements.

The purpose of the learning strategies programme

Because the course was a first year course which provided an introduction to the study of language for a number of programmes of study, Graham wanted to teach learning strategies which were relevant to university studies in general as well as to the study and analysis of languages.

The main aims of the learning strategies programme were to help students be systematic, analytical and critical in their approach to language and to develop their understanding through inquiry and systematic analysis. These aims were to be achieved by using practical work in the analysis of different languages, and by critical observation and analysis of their own and others' speech and writing.

Graham felt that the learning strategies which would support these aims and contribute in a broader way to students' further studies would be those which emphasized the relative importance of various items of information and the interrelationships between these ideas. However, he recognized that even though the strategies would support the learning of linguistic analysis, teaching them would compete for time within the course. As a result he decided to limit the strategies he taught to the following: note making, writing paragraphs, organizing ideas, analysing a question, generating questions and concept mapping.

He integrated the teaching of these strategies with the subject matter of the course by teaching them as they were required by the students. For example, he taught note making from text using material that introduced the study of linguistics. Students then applied this process to their set reading from the text for the following week. He then taught paragraph writing and got students to write paragraphs using notes they made from their text as their source of information. Paragraph and summary writing were incorporated into both of their assignments where there was an emphasis on selecting main points and leaving out redundant information.

Reactions to the learning strategies programme

Successes

Graham felt that the learning strategies he taught in the course were success-ful in increasing student awareness of how to approach their studies in a way that would lead to better learning and understanding. Students improved their skill in using strategies of note making, paragraph writing and organiz-ing ideas, and in the analysis of questions. They seemed better able to identify the main points in a piece of writing and determine the relationships between various supporting ideas.

The inclusion of learning strategies in the course caused Graham to recon-sider the subject matter of the course and its sequence. This resulted in a very different course organization and arrangement of its content. For instance the strategies of note making from text and paragraph writing could not be applied easily to the linguistic analytical techniques which constituted the main content of the course; however they could be related to other elements of the course, because they focused on identifying main points and on developing an argument or exposition. Graham brought forward the read-ing-based component of the course and incorporated paragraph writing in it. Paragraph writing was also applied to other reading and assignments, thus integrating the readings more explicitly into the course. The new sequence of topics and the greater emphasis on reading-based topics rather than analysis seemed to result in a more interesting course.

In a similar way the strategy of organizing ideas was used to clarify students' understanding of basic sentence forms and functions. This informa-tion was scattered through a chapter, so a matrix was used to organize it better. The matrix focused attention on the form-function relationships of the various sentence types and helped students answer an assignment question on indirect speech acts.

Some students clearly appreciated the opportunity to learn these strate-gies. Others were sceptical, including some students in their second year of study who wanted to know whether they could continue to use their own strategies. Graham assured them that this was acceptable, provided the strategies they used were based on principles of effective learning, and students did not just follow a preferred strategy without thinking about how it would affect their learning.

Graham found the attention he gave to learning strategies was a positive experience for himself as well as for the students. The programme made him more conscious of the strategies and techniques involved in the linguistic analysis procedures that formed the course content. This awareness helped him provide more explicit and more adequate coverage of the techniques used to study linguistics.

Graham observed that the attrition rate from the course was lower than in previous years. He took this to indicate that students had a greater sense of competence and interest in the course.

Difficulties

The main difficulty that Graham experienced related to the strategy of note making from text. He felt that the session on this strategy took too long. He also felt that the note making format supplied in Part Two of this book was too rigid and restrictive for use with real materials. He thought it was a useful format to use for introducing note making, but felt that other formats could be developed which would be easier to use and still contain the features that promote learning and understanding.

Students showed some scepticism and resistance to the note making strategy, but Graham thought this was exacerbated by their spending longer on this strategy than planned. Students were also reluctant to reduce a short chapter of the text to a single paragraph following their note making, and seemed unwilling to focus just on the main points.

Graham also had some difficulties with the time that was available to teach the learning strategies. They took longer to teach than he had expected, which made it difficult for him to cover all the course content. Once he became aware of this, he changed his programme and did not teach all the strategies that he had intended.

Graham was hesitant when introducing the note making strategy, for he wondered whether it was too elementary for the students. At the same time he was aware that many students did not make effective notes and had difficulty arriving at the main points and structure of an argument. He felt it was important to emphasize that achieving ends is not tied to one specific note making format, and that a flexible approach was acceptable provided the ends were truly met. His uncertainty may have contributed to the difficulties he experienced in teaching this strategy.

Future directions

Graham intends to make a number of adjustments to the course. He wants to increase the attention paid to learning strategies; he will try to reduce the amount of subject matter contained in the course in order to do so. This will enable him to teach the learning strategies which he had to drop because there was no time, and give students additional practice with the learning strategies which were successful.

He will also review the linguistic analysis component of the course in order to improve the presentation and practice of analysis strategies. This can be seen as an offshoot of the learning strategies programme, since some of the processes used in the learning strategies are essential to analysing and understanding textual material.

Reflections

The learning strategies programme was very useful to me personally in making me think through the role of strategies and the nature of learning – both in relation to general academic work and linguistic analysis. While the introduction of the strategies took longer than suggested by the authors of the materials, this does not nullify the value of teaching them in class. The learning strategies have had some effect in developing the students' ability to learn from written materials, and to determine the main points of a passage and write to the point.

The linking of learning strategies with content seemed to be beneficial. Without such a link it would have been difficult to include the learning strategies, because students would have seen them as irrelevant and time would not have permitted.

Early childhood education

Contributed by Loraine Corrie, Department of Early Childhood Studies

The teacher

Loraine has taught and researched at Edith Cowan University for four years. Before that, she was a lecturer at the University of London Institute of Education. Her main teaching interests are in the area of active learning and cognitive processing. Her research interests are centred around teachers' knowledge, developing collaborative networks between teachers, and early intervention into attention deficit disorder.

The course

Loraine taught in the first year course 'Early Childhood Studies – Education 1', which is part of the Bachelor of Arts in Early Childhood Education. It is a compulsory course in this programme, and focuses on the development of the child from birth to 8 years in the areas of physical, social, cognitive, language and emotional development. The main objective of the course was to introduce students to different theoretical perspectives of development that occur in this age span. Students were encouraged to take a wide view of normal development in order to identify children's needs in an educational setting. To do this they were expected to develop skills in observing and recording this development.

Students attended classes for three hours each week over the 13-week semester. The usual class organization was lectures and tutorials. Students completed three formal assessments: a mid-term test, an observation file and an end of semester examination.

The students

About half of the students in this course came to university directly from secondary school, while the other half were mature students. Almost all students were female. In this particular semester there were 95 female students and only two male students. Some of them expected to work in child-care centres, but most were likely to work with 5–8-year-old children in primary schools. There were 36 students in Loraine's tutorial group.

Students taking this course have usually aimed simply to pass the course. The majority of them focused on meeting requirements and doing as they were told. The background knowledge of the students was mixed. Some students came with practical work experience, some had experience as parents, and some had studied related courses at secondary school. Most students had little formal knowledge of child development and the theories that explain development.

The purpose of the learning strategies programme

Loraine wanted to help students become more active learners by developing a range of effective learning strategies. She also wanted to help them develop positive attitudes and skills so they could work better in collaborative groups.

To achieve these aims, she decided to teach students the following learning strategies: study and time management, identifying main points from lectures and readings, note making from text, writing summaries from notes, note making from lectures, organizing ideas using diagrams and matrices, generating questions, memorizing information, concept mapping, preparing for multiple-choice tests, analysing a question and planning a response, and exam preparation.

She integrated the strategies with the subject matter of the course by teaching the strategies as they were required by the students. Each topic presented in class included at least one learning strategy and accompanying activities to practise using the strategy. The strategies taught early in the course were revised and practised a number of times during the semester. For example, students were taught to make notes from text during the fourth week. They made these notes from their set reading for that week. Note making was referred to again during the semester and was formally retaught in the eighth week, using the set reading. Students were taught to write a paragraph and a summary using their notes. In this way the students learned about note making and summary writing as they carried out the reading needed for their class work and assignments.

Reactions to the learning strategies programme

Successes

Loraine felt that she achieved a number of successes during the semester. One of the strategies that worked well was note making from text. Loraine found that it took longer to teach than she had anticipated, as the students took a lot of time to actually read and make notes. She did not follow all the suggested teaching steps outlined in Part Two of this book. However, when she revised this strategy she used all the steps and observed that students found it easier. Students who continued using the note making strategy subsequently reported that it helped them a great deal.

The students' reaction to the learning strategies programme was most positive. They displayed a better spirit in class and almost all students participated fully in all the activities and discussions. The group work was a particularly positive feature, and students worked together in a more collegial way on meaningful activities.

Loraine felt that one of the successes from this programme was the enjoyment she gained from trying out new teaching strategies and different approaches to teaching. In particular she felt positive about the quality of group work:

I felt different when the students were working in groups. Before I often felt hesitant to join a group because I'd feel I would have to push them along, but this semester the group is so focused and task-oriented that this hasn't been a problem at all.

She felt she would have been more nervous about teaching learning strategies without having the details presented in Part Two of this book and the support of the others involved in the programme. She believes that careful planning before the start of the semester was an essential ingredient that led to the success of her programme:

I think of it like Chinese cooking – it's all in the preparation. My plan has been invaluable, even though I've changed it, a flexible guide.

Difficulties

The main difficulty that Loraine experienced related to time. There were many occasions, especially during the lecture presentations, when she felt that she needed to focus more on the subject matter. This made it difficult to maintain a focus on the learning strategies. The workshops and tutorials were less constrained by time, but she still felt that she was trying to include too much in some sessions. Once Loraine recognized that she was trying to do too much, she did not introduce all the strategies she had planned but focused on revising the strategies that she had already taught:

I did this in the second half of the programme to meet the students' needs, and then I felt less pressured myself. I had been trying to do too much.

Another time-related difficulty arose from differences in the speed at which students worked through various tasks. While some students grasped the ideas quickly, others were much slower. This was particularly evident when teaching the note making strategy, and some students took much longer than she had anticipated:

I've really come to understand how the students' pace varies. I knew this before of course, but I really know now! I think I tend to overestimate what most students can do.

With the group work, time became a different sort of problem in an unexpectedly positive way:

Whereas in the past I've found a two-hour tutorial a long stretch, these tutorials have flown by and I could always use more time. I could easily plan a three-hour session using these strategies, and I'd be sure that the students were involved in valuable learning.

The students were challenged by some strategies, particularly concept mapping and generating questions. Concept mapping was difficult because some students believed there should be a right answer and worried that they may have got it wrong; they had difficulty dealing with uncertainty. Some students also had difficulty generating clear and challenging questions. Loraine intends to provide for consolidation of these strategies in future courses.

An unexpected difficulty occurred because many of the tasks required students to skim read. Students were not skilled at this, and Loraine found it difficult to explain what was involved even though it is something she herself does a great deal. (Following Loraine's comments we have included a section on skim reading in Part Two of this book).

Students benefited from revising the strategies and practising them later in the semester. However, Loraine noticed that they tended to revert to their familiar strategies when they were under stress to submit assignments and study for end of semester examinations in a number of courses. This became obvious when students asked her for sets of notes to help them revise for the examination. Loraine responded by revising the strategy of organizing information by using matrices and tables, and note making strategies.

Loraine felt that some of the difficulties she initially experienced in teaching learning strategies arose from the way she presented them, because she was not always confident or practised in some aspects of the strategies. However, when she retaught the strategies later in the semester she felt more skilled and confident, and experienced fewer difficulties.

Future directions

Loraine believes that she will be less tentative about introducing and teaching learning strategies in future, and will be more active in teaching and modelling them. She commented that as she became more confident teaching the strategies she found that she followed the teaching steps described in Part Two more closely. She believes that the students must be taken through the strategies in a step-by-step way in order to fully understand and be able to use them.

She also intends to introduce fewer strategies into any one course so that she can allow more time to teach, practise and revise them.

Reflections

I am so much happier in tutorials working this way. I never liked the 'now get into small groups and discuss' approach as I did not think it worked well and so I was quite half-hearted about it. I've noticed with these new strategies that I *feel* enthusiastic, and the working buzz in the room has a qualitative difference – certainly the comments of the group have been insightful and perceptive. I'm very happy with their progress. I'm not sure if they are just a great group, but I am sure the programme has made a difference. I have enjoyed meeting with them each week, and have not had the old, dreadful feeling of pushing a barrow uphill.

The class group is more collaborative and collegial than any I've known, and I've taken time to support this when I can. I've talked about the value of study groups, sharing materials, and talking about what they know, and they are doing all of these things.

Accounting

Contributed by Len Therry and Roger Willcocks, Department of Financial Accounting

The teachers

Len has taught and researched at Edith Cowan University for six years. Before that he was a secondary school business teacher and an auditor in chartered accounting. His main teaching interests are in the area of accounting and literacy. His research interests are centred around social semiotics and accounting education, and tertiary literacy.

Roger has taught and researched at Edith Cowan University for two years. Before that he was a senior lecturer at Plymouth Polytechnic and a lecturer at Massey University. His main teaching interests are in the areas of accounting theory and financial and management accounting. His research interests are centred around case study research.

The course

Len and Roger taught in the first-year course 'Accounting 1', which is a compulsory foundation course in the Bachelor of Business. It is the first of a series of courses in accounting for students who intend to major in accounting, but it might be the only accounting course taken by students who major in another area. The course focused on developing understandings and technical skills associated with fundamental aspects of accounting.

Students attended classes for three hours each week during the 13-week semester, comprising a two-hour lecture and a one-hour tutorial. They completed three assessment tasks: an essay on accounting practice, an assignment that required them to apply accounting processes to financial data, and an examination. The course was taught on two metropolitan campuses and a country campus about 200km distant. The course has a large enrolment each semester, so Len and Roger worked with five other tutors to take the tutorials.

The students

Students varied greatly in background and experience. Some came to university directly from secondary school, but others had been in the workforce for some years. Some had already studied accounting at school or had some experience of it at work, but it was a completely new field of study for others. A significant number of overseas students took the course, and most of them spoke English as a second language. Some students took the course only because it was a compulsory foundation course in their degree, and they wanted just to pass it with as little effort as possible. Others took it because they intended to major in accounting, and wanted to understand the principles and become proficient in the processes of accounting.

Many of the younger students seemed content to use a surface approach to learning, so that they focused on learning facts and procedures that were necessary to satisfy the assessment requirements of the course. The older students were more likely to see learning as qualitative and to focus on trying to understand the subject matter.

Len and Roger's experience in teaching this course led them to believe that many students came into the course without much knowledge of the strategies that would help them learn the subject matter with understanding and achieve the objectives of the course.

The purpose of the learning strategies programme

Len and Roger wanted to teach some strategies in the context of the accounting course that would help their students become more proficient learners. They wanted to encourage the students to adopt a deeper approach to their learning, and focus more on understanding the subject matter and less on reproducing it. They also wanted students to realize that accounting involved communication between people as well as processing of data. To help them achieve these goals they decided to teach students the following strategies: using study groups, analysing a question and planning a response, study and time management, note making from text, explaining ideas, and learning from feedback. They recognized that if they were to be successful they would have to teach the strategies in a way that allowed students to see their relevance and encouraged them to use the strategies in their learning. So, they decided to make the classes more interactive and more student-centred than before, and they encouraged tutors to take a personal interest in the students in order to enhance motivation and stimulate interest.

They recognized that it would be difficult to cover both the strategies and subject matter in a one-hour tutorial, so they made some changes to the way that tutorials were conducted. Previously in the tutorial sessions students worked on accounting problems and explored solutions to them. This was changed by placing solutions to the problems in the closed reserve section of the library. Students were expected to complete the set questions in their own time, compare their solutions with those in the library, and then raise any questions or issues with the tutor. Getting students to use their own time to complete tasks that had previously been done in class meant that time was available to teach the learning strategies in the tutorials.

Len and Roger integrated the strategies with the subject matter of the course by teaching the strategies when they were needed by the students. Some strategies were taught in the lecture sessions by the lead lecturer, while others were taught in tutorials. This created a special challenge, because tutors who had not expressed any commitment to teaching learning strategies and who had not received any special training in how to teach them were required to teach them in the first week of classes. To help them do this, Len and Roger prepared teaching packages for each tutorial session that described how the tutors should conduct the session, and worked with the tutors each week to ensure that they understood the materials and felt comfortable with the teaching and learning activities.

Reactions to the learning strategies programme

Successes

In general, instruction in the learning strategies seemed to be successful, particularly with respect to using study groups, note making from text, and explaining ideas. Using study groups was taught in the tutorials in the first week. The team found that it was an appropriate strategy to teach at this time: it gave students an opportunity to get to know each other better and do some initial planning to support each other in their learning. Staff arranged for a room to be designated as a meeting place on a particular afternoon each week, so that students in the course could meet to study together or just make contact with other students taking the course. Explaining ideas was presented in the fifth week, and was linked with these study groups. Students practised using the strategy by explaining accounting concepts to their peers. While they were doing this they were actively learning about accounting. Note making was also well received, and some students acknowledged that they needed to learn a framework for making notes. Students practised making notes with material from their accounting textbook.

Len and Roger believe that they succeeded in making classes more inter-active and student-centred. While the learning strategies were being taught, both tutors and students were actively involved in a process of cooperative learning, and shared the responsibility for teaching and learning. Classes seemed to be more interactive than before and tutors took more personal interest in the students.

Student reaction to the programme was generally positive, and students reported that they could see the benefits of the programme. The older students seemed to benefit more than younger students. Some students who were repeating the course after having failed it in a previous semester expressed appreciation about the new way the course was conducted.

Len and Roger believed that the programme was beneficial to the students and helped them cope better with the demands of the course. They also found the programme to be personally satisfying and rewarding from a teaching perspective. However, they believe that they tried to do too much in the context of one course, and that they should not have tried to teach all the strategies they selected.

They would like teachers in other foundation courses to participate in the programme so that a more coordinated approach could be used to teach learning strategies. This would have the advantage of spreading the load and presenting students with a consistent message that learning strategies are important.

The tutors had mixed reactions to the programme. They were generally supportive of the programme and thought that it could have a significant effect on student learning. However, they were not all convinced that it actually produced an improvement in the quality of student work, and expressed concern that the time spent on strategy instruction reduced the time that was available to work on the subject matter.

Difficulties
Len and Roger found that the programme was difficult to implement, partly because they tried to achieve so much in one semester. One of the major purposes of the course was to teach students the fundamentals of accounting principles, which can be built on in later courses. As a result the course

contained a lot of subject matter and made heavy demands on teachers if they were to cover this in the available time. With the inclusion of the learning strategies programme, staff found themselves trying to use the one-hour tutorial to cover both a learning strategy and a technical accounting issue, each of which might require one hour to present. Consequently some tutorials became rushed and more teacher-centred than was planned, and tutors found it difficult not to give priority to the accounting subject matter.

Another difficulty was caused by the involvement of so many sessional tutors in the course. None of them had participated in the decision to run the programme or been trained in its rationale and methods, so before each class they had to be briefed on the particular learning strategy and how to teach it. This was threatening to some of them, and time-consuming for all. Some of the tutors were apprehensive about whether they would be successful in the programme, and were concerned that they might not be seen to be devoting enough time to working with the subject matter.

Future directions

Len and Roger acknowledged that they should not have expected a programme conducted in one course of study to have a large effect on students' learning. However, they believe that they can make some contribution to change, and that it is worthwhile trying to do this. Their belief is supported by recent reports on accounting education which argue for a shift in emphasis from one that is knowledge-based to one that focuses on the learning process. They intend to develop and repeat the programme and hope to get support from other teachers in their department. They would like to review the content of the course and see whether they can reduce the amount of subject matter it contains. They acknowledge that they will have to spend more time with the tutors to convince them of the worth of the programme and ensure they are confident that they will not disadvantage the students.

Reflections

I am very excited about what we are doing here, and can appreciate the benefits of what we are doing to make students more effective learners. I found the learning strategies programme to be beneficial to the students and rewarding from a teaching perspective.

Information science

Contributed by Jan Ring, Department of Library and Information Science

The teacher

Jan has taught and researched at Edith Cowan University for 12 years. Before that she was a secondary school teacher. Her main teaching interests are in the area of multimedia and library technologies. Her research interests are centred on human–computer interactions and alternative delivery modes for education. One of her achievements is the establishment of the university's 'Virtual Campus', which is a computer-based communication system that allows students throughout the world to access a variety of university resources by using a modem and personal computer.

The course

Jan taught in the first year course 'Information Agencies and Environments', which is part of the Associate Diploma of Science (Information Technology). The course focused on developing an awareness of the various information agencies and environments available in the community and on the role of communication technology in information transfer. Students attended class for four hours each week, which included lectures, computer workshops and structured visits to libraries and information agencies. They also participated in a two-week practicum. They completed three assessment tasks: a tutorial presentation, a report on their visits to the various agencies, and a practicum report.

The course was offered by distance education as well as on campus. At the beginning of the semester, the external, or distance education, students received a package of materials which included readings and a study guide. They worked through these materials on an independent basis under Jan's guidance. In addition to the assessment activities already mentioned, the external students had to sit for an examination at the end of semester.

The students

Only about 10 per cent of students in this course were immediate school-leavers. Most were mature women who were returning to study after raising a family or spending some years in the workforce. Many had enrolled in the Associate Diploma instead of a full degree because they were not sure of their ability to handle a three-year degree. They did not find the subject matter of the course particularly difficult. However, since they took the course in their first semester at university, they often had difficulty coming to terms with the various demands of being a student and integrating them with their family responsibilities.

Jan believed that many of these students held quantitative conceptions of learning and teaching and saw their learning role as memorizing information that was presented to them by the teacher.

The purpose of the learning strategies programme

Jan identified a number of problems that she wanted to address. Students had indicated that they wanted to learn to manage their time more effectively. Some of them wanted to learn more about study skills, but others indicated that they could get this kind of help from their partners, friends, or from university staff. However, the external students found it difficult to get help in this way, and wanted help with several aspects of their learning, including writing essays, understanding what an assignment or examination question requires, writing critically rather than descriptively, and handling examinations.

Jan wanted to help the on-campus students adjust to the university environment so that they could make the most of the available learning opportunities. She also wanted them to accept responsibility for their own learning and adopt a more active and independent approach to their learning. In order to achieve these intentions, she decided to teach them the following learning strategies: time management, using study groups, making notes from readings, writing summaries, analysing a question, generating questions, and assignment preparation.

She integrated these strategies with the subject matter of the course by teaching the strategies at an appropriate time in the context of the subject matter or assessment task that students were working on at the time. For example in the first week she focused on personal organization and time management. Students used a semester planner (see 'Study and time management' in Chapter 10) for their long-term planning and developed a detailed schedule of activities for the coming week. She arranged for the class to form support groups comprising students in similar circumstances, such as mothers with young children, or single students with part-time employment. She believed that forming groups containing students with similar interests and circumstances would enable them to provide better support for each other.

Jan also wanted to cater for the needs of the external students, but this was more difficult. These students worked with materials that had been prepared before the semester began. The materials could not be modified at short notice to incorporate a special programme. However, some of the students were able to use the university's 'Virtual Campus'. One of the features of the 'Virtual Campus' system is a 'Chat' facility which allows staff and students to communicate with one another in real time by sending notes across the computer network. Jan decided to use this facility to teach some learning strategies to students who wished to participate on a voluntary basis. She posted material electronically to students so they could read it in advance and then work on it during the tutorial. During the tutorial she clarified the strategies and students shared their reactions and experiences with each other. After the session she posted a transcript of the tutorial on an electronic notice board on the 'Virtual Campus' so that other students could read about the tutorial. She originally intended to offer three tutorial sessions on the 'Virtual Campus' to experiment with the process. However, the demand from students was so great that this grew to five formal sessions and several informal sessions. About eight students participated regularly in these sessions.

Reactions to the learning strategies programme

Successes
The learning strategies programme for the on-campus students seemed to be successful. The support groups that students established in the first week stayed together and were useful in providing students with informal help with personal difficulties and assistance with study, planning and writing. The most successful group was probably the 'Mothers with older children' group that became a study group in which students worked together on assignments and other aspects of their learning.

Students seemed to become more active in their learning, and more willing to raise issues, provide information and collect materials to support the subject matter. They also used the skills gained in the programme to organize their workload and to make more efficient use of their time.

Students reacted differently to the programme according to their age. The older students were generally pleased to be involved, and perceived the learning strategy instruction as timely and useful. They were willing to comment on the process, try out the new strategies, and give feedback on how they used them. The younger students were quite different. They seemed confident about their ability to handle the course without changing the way they used learning strategies. They cooperated in class, but did not seem to think much about how they could use the strategies or apply them to their other courses of study. These younger students also received the lowest marks in the course.

The most enthusiastic response came from the external students, who sometimes feel isolated and usually respond positively to special attempts to cater for their needs. To some extent their enthusiasm may reflect their voluntary participation in the programme. They had to give up their own time to participate in the tutorial sessions in which the learning strategies were taught, whereas the on-campus students had no choice and participated during regular class time.

Jan found that, as the programme developed, she became more aware of how much students needed to learn about effective learning strategies, and she felt satisfaction at being able to address some of these needs. She also found that her conception of teaching changed as she began to focus more on helping students learn the subject matter and less on just presenting material for them to learn.

Difficulties

The main difficulty that Jan experienced related to time. With the on-campus students, teaching the learning strategies took up time that she would otherwise have spent on the subject matter of the course. This meant that she often had to rush through the material so that students did not have enough time to work with it properly.

Time was also a problem with the external students. It was difficult to arrange time to prepare and conduct the on-line tutorials, because it was an extra commitment both for her and the students. She had to prepare material and post it electronically in time for students to capture it so that they could work on it during the tutorial. Each tutorial then required at least one hour on the system. After the session she had to edit the transcript of the tutorial and post it on the study skills notice board on the 'Virtual Campus'. She also had to deal with contacts from students who sent questions and comments by e-mail. Overall, she found that teaching a strategy on-line required much more time than teaching it on-campus.

Jan also took some time to adjust to teaching on the computer system. She found it disconcerting not to be able to see the students and receive non-verbal feedback from them. It was also difficult for her to determine how they were reacting to her instruction and what impact she was having on their understanding.

She found that the younger on-campus students seemed unaware that they should work on their learning strategies. They believed that they would manage quite well in the course and did not need to consider new ways of going about their learning, especially if this required them to put in more time and effort.

Teaching learning strategies in this way required Jan to be well organized and well prepared. Each activity had to be thought out, carefully prepared and presented. In particular, she found that she overestimated the skill level of her students, and found herself trying to teach higher level skills to students who were weak on the fundamentals. In future she will try to give students some informal tasks that will indicate how well they can perform fundamental skills such as constructing sentences and writing paragraphs. She also intends to develop a wider repertoire of teaching skills and strategies in order to cope with the new demands placed on her.

Future directions

Jan intends to review the assessment provisions of the course. The assessments required students to report on their observations and did not encourage critical thinking. The timing of the assessments was also problematic, since the only item that required extended writing was submitted at the end of semester, when it was too late to show students how to correct any weaknesses that were identified in their writing. In future she will integrate a few small pieces of non-assessable work into the programme so that she can assess current skill levels, give students feedback and look for improvements in their work.

With the external students, she intends to develop a learning strategies programme and advertise it before the semester begins. Students will have to register for the classes, and will be sent a set of materials that will be used in the programme to teach them the various learning strategies. She will then be able to focus the on-line tutorials on clarifying understanding and developing skill in using the learning strategies. She will explore the possibility of supplementing the on-line classes with a teleconference which will allow students to talk to each other over the telephone network.

She would like to achieve more with the young students who have come to university direct from secondary school. They seem less aware than the older students that they could enhance their learning by working on their learning strategies. She intends to make a special effort to demonstrate to them that their learning strategies are not meeting their needs and university requirements, and that it would be worth their while to spend time and effort in learning new strategies.

Reflections

I'm utterly convinced of the worth of this programme, particularly for the external students. Despite the demands it has made on my time in getting material out to them, setting up on-line tutorials, running the tutorials and so on, it has been worth it. I want to do this again, and do it better.

Conclusions from the case studies

Student reactions

Most students reacted positively to being taught learning strategies in the context of their regular coursework. Indeed, many students wondered why this did not happen in other classes. However, it was common for some students to resist being taught learning strategies when they were first presented. One reason for this is that they saw themselves as successful learners who were already skilled at learning. Another reason is that they believed that strategy instruction took up time that should be devoted to teaching the subject matter of the course. A third reason is that strategy instruction requires students to apply more effort than would be needed if they were just presented with material to learn and reproduce when required.

To minimize resistance from students it is important to remind them that they are learning the subject matter at the same time as they are learning and practising the strategies. It is also important to get them to evaluate the strategies that they normally use, and compare them with those that you are teaching. If they see that the new methods are better than those they normally use, they are more likely to respond positively to the programme. In Part Two of this book we indicated how you can get students to evaluate the effectiveness of the strategies that they use.

Teacher reactions

The teachers responded enthusiastically to teaching learning strategies in the context of their regular instruction. They found that it changed their way of viewing teaching, and their conceptions of teaching became less focused on presenting information and more on helping students learn with understanding. They found that their classes became more interactive, and students were more interested in the subject matter and more enthusiastic about their learning. All of the teachers in our programme intend to continue teaching in this way.

Time requirements

It was common for teachers to underestimate how much time was needed to teach the strategies properly. This caused them to rush the teaching, so that some students did not learn how to use the strategies properly.

Teaching learning strategies takes time. Teachers have to establish a need for the strategy, explain it to students, and convince them that it is better than the strategy they normally use. They then have to teach students how to use the strategy, and get them to practise using it. They also have to teach students when and where to use the various strategies.

The steps we have developed for teaching learning strategies cover all these aspects of strategy instruction. We believe that it is necessary to follow all the steps, and if steps are omitted to save time, the quality of teaching and learning may be reduced.

Integration of strategies with subject matter

Some teachers had difficulty fully integrating the learning strategies with the subject matter. One aspect of integration is to teach the strategies in the context of the course, and encourage students to use them in appropriate circumstances. Another aspect is to teach the strategies at the most appropriate time: for instance when students are most likely to recognize a need for them. However, integration also involves realizing that effective teaching requires both teaching and learning processes, and that a focus on only one of these processes is inadequate. It takes some time before teachers and students accept this. At first teachers see teaching learning strategies and teaching subject matter as separate tasks. It is at this time that they are most likely to feel that strategy instruction is taking time away from the subject matter. However, once they realize that effective teaching should involve teaching about learning as well as teaching about subject matter, they are less likely to see this as a problem.

Confidence in teaching learning strategies

Most of the teachers with whom we worked reported that they were uncertain and tentative when they first taught learning strategies. They were more accustomed to teaching subject matter, and normally assumed that students had the necessary skills and strategies to be able to learn it effectively. They also felt that students expected to be treated like skilful learners, and wanted to be taught subject matter rather than learning processes. However, as these teachers worked with their students on learning strategies, they became aware that many students were not as skilful as they had believed. At the same time, the students were pleased that the teachers were helping them become more effective learners, and gave this feedback to the teachers. This made the teachers more confident about the benefits of teaching learning strategies that were integrated with the subject matter.

The importance of planning

Thorough planning is needed for success in teaching learning strategies. One important task is to plan to teach the strategies when students are most likely to be responsive to strategy instruction. For example, teaching students how to plan an assignment is often best done when they start work on their first assignment. On the other hand, some students may respond better if this strategy is taught after they have already completed an assignment and are looking for a better way to manage the task. For these students it might be better to teach the strategy when they are starting work on their second assignment.

A second task is to plan to link strategy instruction with the most appropriate subject matter. For example, when teaching note making from text, it is important to start with fairly easy text that is clearly structured and has fairly obvious main points. Not all topics in a course will have readings that meet this requirement.

A final aspect of planning relates to the process that is used for teaching the strategy. The teaching steps we have developed for each strategy clearly describe how this can be done. However, even though these steps are clearly detailed, teachers found that it was important to prepare thoroughly so that they fully understood the nature and purpose of each step, and could teach the strategy with confidence.

Chapter 14:

Developing and Implementing a Programme to Teach Learning Strategies

The university teachers who participated in our programme found that it was necessary to engage in thorough planning before teaching learning strategies in the context of a regular course of instruction. They also found it necessary to monitor the programme so that they could make changes and address difficulties as they arose. Here we provide some suggestions that will help you develop and implement a programme. We present this under headings developed from those we use when teaching students to use a systematic approach to their learning: identifying and clarifying the task, developing a programme, monitoring progress, and checking the outcomes of the programme.

Identifying and clarifying the task

An obvious starting point is to identify the learning strategies that you want to teach. One way of doing this is to examine the course and determine what learning strategies students need in order to manage the course successfully. For example, if the course involves mass lectures, you may wish to teach students how to make notes from lectures. If the course requires students to coordinate and integrate information from various sources, you may wish to teach strategies for organizing information.

Another way of identifying appropriate learning strategies is to think about what the students were like when you taught this course or level of student before. What learning strategies did they use well? What learning strategies did they not use well? What learning strategies would have helped them learn better?

You may identify many strategies that you wish to teach. However, we suggest that you start by teaching only a few. Several of the teachers we worked with indicated that their programme would have worked better if they had planned to teach fewer strategies. On the first occasion that you teach learning strategies in the context of a regular course of instruction, it is probably best to restrict yourself to about four or five strategies. This will allow you to allocate enough time to teach them and leave you with time to revise and practise them.

Another important aspect of clarifying the task is for you to think about the expectations that students have of the course, and the conceptions of learning that they hold. These will affect the success of your programme. For example, some students will hold quantitative conceptions of learning and expect you to present them with information that they can memorize and reproduce. You will encounter resistance if you try to teach these students learning strategies that focus on working with information in order to develop deeper understanding of the subject matter. If student expectations and conceptions of learning do not match your intentions, you will have to plan to deal with the mismatch in some way. This may involve you in working with the students at the beginning of semester to clarify and redirect their expectations. In the section 'Clarifying expectations with students' in Chapter 11 we describe how you can do this.

Developing the programme

Developing the programme involves two main tasks: locating the learning strategies into your course, and checking that the course is presented in a way that encourages students to use the strategies. With respect to locating the learning strategies, you should try to teach them when students are most likely to need to use them, and when students can see clearly how they can use them to help their learning. For example, you could teach students how to make notes for assignments when they are beginning to work on the first assignment in the course. You could teach them to construct concept maps when you have them review their knowledge about a particular topic, such as at the end of a major section of work.

You should also check that the course is arranged in a way that encourages students to use the strategies that you teach. As indicated in Part One of this book, students will not use learning strategies unless they believe that it is necessary to do so. They will not work with information to develop understanding if the course only requires them to memorize and reproduce information.

Monitoring progress

It is important to monitor the implementation of your programme and student reaction to it. As indicated in some of the case studies, you may find that you have to make some changes to your plan. You might have tried to do too much, or you might have to give students more practice on a particular strategy than you had expected. You might have to change your expectations of students. This happened with some of the teachers with whom we worked, who were hesitant about teaching the learning strategies because they thought that students already knew how to use them. In fact, the students were not as skilful as they thought. You might have to change the way you intended to teach the strategies. This happened with teachers who omitted some of the steps recommended for teaching particular strategies, because they wanted to save time. They later found that this resulted in their students not being able to use the strategy properly.

An important aspect of monitoring the programme is to get feedback from your students on a regular basis. In the section 'Getting feedback from students' in Chapter 11 we describe how you can do this. You might also examine some samples of student work to determine how well students are using the strategies that you teach. For example, if you teach them a particular way of making notes from their reading, you might examine notes they make on a set reading. This will allow you to determine whether you need to provide further instruction on this method of making notes, or whether you need to change some aspect of the course to encourage students to use the strategy.

Checking the outcomes of the programme

As the semester comes to an end, you should check on the outcomes of your programme. Even if you have been getting feedback on a regular basis during the semester, it is important to get feedback at the end. It is only at this time that students can make an overall summative judgement about the programme, and give you feedback on how the various components of the course fitted together and affected their learning, and whether they liked the process.

You might wish to compare the standard of work achieved by students in your programme with that achieved by similar students who were not taught learning strategies. While it would be satisfying if students in your programme achieved better results, you should not be disappointed if this does not happen. Changing students' learning behaviour is a slow process, and the benefits may not be immediately obvious. Even if students use the strategies effectively, they will not obtain higher grades unless the assessment system rewards students who show deeper levels of understanding. As we indicated in Part One, this is often not the case.

Finally, you should reflect on your own reactions to the programme, and make plans for the future. Although you can do this by yourself, you will probably find it helpful to discuss your programme with an interested colleague who can support and encourage your efforts. Teachers in our programme concluded that their efforts had been successful, and reported that their approach to teaching had changed. They found that they focused less on presenting information, and more on helping students learn with understanding. Perhaps the best indicator of their success was their intention to repeat the programme next semester, and to do it better.

References

Ames, C (1992) 'Classrooms: Goals, structures and student motivation', *Journal of Educational Psychology*, **84**, 261–71.

Angelo, T and Cross, K P (1993) *Classroom Assessment Techniques: A handbook for college teachers*, San Francisco, CA: Jossey-Bass.

Atkinson, R C and Shiffrin, R M (1968) 'Human memory: A proposed system and its control processes', in K Spence and J Spence (eds) *The Psychology of Learning and Motivation* (Vol 2), New York: Academic Press.

Aulich, T (1990) *Priorities for Reform in Higher Education*. Report by the Senate Standing Committee on Employment, Education and Training, Canberra: Australian Government Publishing Service.

Barry, K and King, L (1993) *Beginning Teaching* (2nd edn), Sydney: Social Science Press.

Biggs, J B (1987) *Student Approaches to Learning and Studying*, Hawthorn, Victoria: Australian Council for Educational Research.

Biggs, J B (1993a) 'What do inventories of students' learning processes really measure? A theoretical review and clarification', *British Journal of Educational Psychology*, **63**, 3–19.

Biggs, J B (1993b) 'From theory to practice: A cognitive systems approach', *Higher Education Research and Development*, **12**, 73–85.

Biggs, J B and Moore, P J (1993) *The Process of Learning* (3rd edn), Sydney: Prentice-Hall.

Biggs, J B and Telfer, R (1987) *The Process of Learning* (2nd edn), Sydney: Prentice-Hall.

Brown, A L and Campione, J C (1990) 'Communities of learning and thinking, or a context by any other name', in D Kuhn (ed) *Developmental Perspectives in Teaching and Learning Thinking Skills: Contributions to human development* (pp.108–26), Basel: Kargel.

Brown, A L and Day, J D (1983) 'Macrorules for summarising texts: The development of expertise', *Journal of Verbal Learning and Verbal Behaviour*, **22**, 1–14.

Brown, A L, Bransford, J D, Ferrara, R A and Campione, J C (1983) 'Learning, remembering and understanding', in P H Mussen (ed), *Handbook of Child Psychology, Vol 3*. (4th edn, pp.77–166), New York: John Wiley & Sons.

Brown, G and Atkins, N (1988) *Effective Teaching in Higher Education*, London: Methuen.

Burdess, N (1991) *The Handbook of Student Skills*, Sydney: Prentice-Hall.

Campione, J C, Brown, A L and Connell, M L (1989) 'Metacognition: On the importance of understanding what you are doing', in R I Charles and E Silver (eds) *Teaching and Assessing Mathematical Problem Solving*, Reston, VA: National Council of Teachers of Mathematics.

Candy, P C, Crebert, G and O'Leary, J (1994) *Developing Lifelong Learners through Undergraduate Education*, Commissioned Report No. 28. National Board of Employment, Education and Training, Australian Government Publishing Service.

Cawley, P (1989) 'The introduction of a problem-based option into a conventional engineering degree course', *Studies in Higher Education*, **14**, 83–94.

Chalmers, D (1994) 'Local and overseas students' goals and management of study', *Issues in Educational Research*, **4**(2), 25–56.

Chalmers, D (1995) *Improving the Quality of Student Learning through Self-directed Learning and Study Materials*, Vols 1 and 2, Perth: Edith Cowan University.

Chalmers, D and Fuller, R (1994) *Students' Conceptions of Learning and Approaches to Learning in TAFE and University Contexts*, Perth: Edith Cowan University.

Chalmers, D and Lawrence, J A (1993) 'Investigating the effects of planning aids on adults' and adolescents' organization of a complex task', *International Journal of Behavioral Development*, **16**, 191–214.

Chalmers, D, Fuller, R and Kirkpatrick, D (1994) 'Everyone wants an A – but will they even get a C?', paper presented at the annual conference of the Australian Association of Research in Education, Fremantle, Western Australia.

Chalmers, D, Kirkpatrick, D and Fuller, R (1992) *Tertiary Students' Goals, Study Strategies and Management of Study*, University Research Project, Edith Cowan University.

Clift, J C and Imrie, B W (1981) *Assessing Students, Appraising Teaching*, Beckenham: Croon Helm.

Cloete, N and Shochet, I (1986) 'Alternatives to the behavioural technicist conception of study skills', *Higher Education*, **15**, 247–58.

Conway, R, Kember, D, Sivan, A and Wu, M (1993) 'Peer assessment of an individual's contribution to a group project', *Assessment and Evaluation in Higher Education*, **18**, 45–56.

Cooper, G (1994) *Learning to Learn: An introduction to tertiary studies. Learning skills guide #1*, University of Western Australia Student Support Services.

Crooks, T J (1988) 'The impact of classroom evaluation practices on students', *Review of Educational Research,* **58**, 438–81.

Dahlgren, L O (1984) 'Outcomes of learning', in F Marton *et al.*(eds) *The Experience of Learning,* Edinburgh: Scottish Academic Press.

Dansereau, D F (1985) 'Learning strategy research', in J W Segal, S F Chipman and R Glaser (eds) *Thinking and Learning Skills,* Vol. 1 (pp.209–40). Hillsdale, NJ: Erlbaum.

Dansereau, D F (1988) 'Cooperative learning strategies', in C E Weinstein, E T Goetz and P A Alexander (eds) *Learning and Study Strategies: Issues in assessment, instruction and evaluation* (pp.103–20), San Diego, CA: Academic Press.

Dawkins, J. (1987) *Higher Education: A policy discussion paper,* Canberra: Australian Government Publishing Service.

Derry, S J and Murphy, D A (1986) 'Designing systems that train learning ability: From theory to practice', *Review of Educational Research,* **56**, 1–39.

Edith Cowan University (1994) *Vision 2002: A century of achievement – since 1902,* Perth, WA: Edith Cowan University.

Eggen, P D and Kauchak, D (1992) *Educational Psychology: Classroom connections,* New York: Merrill.

Eizenberg, N (1988) 'Approaches to learning anatomy', in P Ramsden (ed) *Improving Learning: New perspectives,* London: Kogan Page.

Farnham-Diggory, S (1972) *Cognitive Processes in Education: A psychological preparation for teaching and curriculum development,* New York: Harper & Row.

Fuller, R, Chalmers, D and Kirkpatrick, D (1993) *Investigating University Students' Learning and Study Strategies: A comparative study of student learning,* ARC Research Project: Edith Cowan University.

Fuller, R, Chalmers, D and Kirkpatrick, D (1995) 'Teaching university students learning and study strategies in context: an experimental study', Research and Development in Higher Education, HERDSA, **17**, 139–61.

Gagné, R M (1985) *The Conditions of Learning* (4th edn), New York: Holt, Rinehart and Winston.

Gaskins, I and Elliot, T (1991) *Implementing Cognitive Strategy Instruction across the School: The benchmark manual for teachers,* Cambridge, MA: Brookline Books.

Gibbs, G (1992) *Improving the Quality of Student Learning,* Bristol: Technical and Education Services.

Gibbs, G and Habeshaw, T (1988) *Preparing to Teach: An introduction to effective teaching in higher education,* Bristol: Technical and Educational Services.

Gleason, M (1985) 'Ten best on learning: A bibliography of essential sources for instructors', *College Teaching,* **33** (1), 8–10.

Goldfinch, J and Raeside, R (1990) 'Development of a peer assessment technique for obtaining individual marks on a group project', *Assessment and Evaluation in Higher Education*, **15**, 210–31.

Gow, L and Kember, D (1993) 'Conceptions of teaching and their relationship to student learning', *British Journal of Educational Psychology*, **63**, 20–33.

King, A (1990) 'Enhancing peer interaction and learning in the classroom through reciprocal questioning', *American Educational Research Journal*, **27**, 664–87.

King, A (1992) 'Comparison of self-questioning, summarizing, and note-taking review as strategies for learning from lectures', *American Education Research Journal*, **29**, 303–23.

Lawrence, J A, Chalmers, D and Pears, H E (1989) 'Promoting students' note-taking skills', *Australian Journal of Reading*, **12**(1), 22–30.

Lawrence, J A and Chalmers, D (1989) *A Notetaking Scheme for Classroom Use: Instructional system*, Technical Report, University of Melbourne, Parkville.

Lindsay, P H and Norman, D A (1977) *Human Information Processing. An introduction to psychology* (2nd edn), New York: Academic Press.

McKeachie, W J (1987) 'The new look in instructional psychology: Teaching strategies for learning and thinking', in E DeCorte, H Lodewijks, R Parmetier and P Span (eds) *Learning and Instruction: European research in an international context* (Vol 1), Oxford: Pergamon Press.

McKeachie, W J, Pintrich, P R, Lin, Y and Smith, D A (1987) *Teaching and Learning in the College Classroom: A review of the research literature*, University of Michigan: NCRIPTAL.

Marton, F and Ramsden, P (1987) 'Learning skills, or skill in learning', in J T Richardson, M W Eysenck and D W Piper (eds) *Student Learning: Research in education and cognitive psychology*, Buckingham: SRME and Open University.

Marton, F and Säljö, R (1984) 'Approaches to learning', in F Marton *et al.* (eds) *The Experience of Learning*, Edinburgh: Scottish Academic Press.

Marton, F, dall'Alba, G and Beaty, E (1993) 'Conceptions of learning', *International Journal of Educational Research*, **19**, 277–300.

Newble, D and Cannon, R (1989) *A Handbook for Teachers in Universities and Colleges*, New York: St Martin's Press.

Nisbet, J and Shucksmith, J (1986) *Learning Strategies*, London: Routledge and Kegan Paul.

Nist, S L, Simpson, M L, Olejenik, S and Mealey, D L (1991) 'The relation between self-selected study processes and test performance', *American Educational Research Journal*, **28**, 849–74.

Norman, D (1976) *Memory and Attention*, New York: Wiley.

Norman, D (1982) *Learning and Memory*, San Francisco, CA: Freeman.

Novak, J D and Gowin, D B (1984) *Learning how to Learn*, Cambridge: Cambridge University Press.

Paris, S G, Lipson, M Y and Wixson, K K (1983) 'Becoming a strategic reader', *Contemporary Educational Psychology*, **8**, 293–316.

Pauk, W (1989) *How to Study in College*, Boston, Mass: Houghton Mifflin.

Peper, R and Mayer, R (1986) 'Generative effects of note-taking during science lectures', *Journal of Educational Psychology*, **78**, 34–8.

Piaget, J (1950) *The Psychology of Intelligence*, London: Routledge and Kegan Paul.

Polya, G (1957) *How to Solve It: A new aspect of mathematical method* (2nd edn), Princeton, NJ: Princeton University Press.

Pressley, M, Borkowski, J G and O'Sullivan, J T (1984) 'Memory strategy instruction is made of this: Metamemory and durable strategy use', *Educational Psychologist*, **19**, 94–107.

Pressley, M, El-Dinary, P B and Brown, R (1992) 'Skilled and not-so-skilled reading: Good information processing and not-so-good information processing', in M Pressley, K R Harris and J T Guthrie (eds) *Promoting Academic Competence and Literacy: Cognitive research and instructional innovation* (pp.91–127), San Diego, CA: Academic Press.

Pressley, M and McCormick, C (1995) *Cognition, Teaching and Assessment*, New York: HarperCollins College Publishers.

Pressley, M, Wood, E, Woloshyn, V E, Martin, V, King, A and Menke, D (1992) 'Encouraging mindful use of prior knowledge: Attempting to construct explanatory answers facilitates learning', *Educational Psychologist*, **27**, 91–109.

Puhl, L and Day, B (1992) *Writing at University: A guide to writing academic essays and reports at Edith Cowan University*, Perth: Edith Cowan University.

Raaheim, A (1984) 'Can students be taught to study? An evaluation of a study-skill programme directed at first year students at the University of Bergen', *Scandinavian Journal of Educational Research*, **28**, 9–15.

Rabinowitz, M, Freeman, K and Cohen, S (1992) 'Use and maintenance of strategies: The influence of accessibility on knowledge', *Journal of Educational Psychology*, **84**, 211–18.

Ramsden, P (1992) *Learning to Teach in Higher Education*, London: Routledge.

Ramsden, P, Beswick, D G and Bowden, J A (1986) 'Effects of learning skills interventions on first year university students' learning', *Human Learning*, **5**, 151–64.

Säljö, R (1979) *Learning in the Learner's Perspective: Some commonsense conceptions*, Reports from the Institute of Education, University of Gotenbörg, No 76.

Salomon, G and Globerson, T (1987) 'Skills may not be enough: The role of mindfulness in learning and transfer', *International Journal of Educational Research*, **11**, 623–34.

Samuelowicz, K (1987) 'Learning problems of overseas students: Two sides of a story', *Higher Education Research and Development*, **6**, 121–33.

Samuelowicz, K and Bain, J (1992) 'Conceptions of teaching held by academic teachers', *Higher Education*, **24**, 93–111.

Scardamalia, M and Bereiter, C (1986) 'Research on written composition', in M C Wittrock (ed.), *Handbook of Research on Teaching* (3rd edn), London: Macmillan.

Shuell, T J (1986) 'Cognitive conceptions of learning', *Review of Educational Research*, **56**, 411–36.

Shuell, T J (1990) 'Phases of meaningful learning', *Review of Educational Research*, **60**, 531–47.

Slavin, R E (1983) *Cooperative Learning*, New York: Longman.

Snyder, B and Pressley, M (1990) 'Introduction to cognitive strategy instruction', in M Pressley and Associates (eds) *Cognitive Strategy Instruction that Really Improves Children's Academic Performance*, Cambridge, Mass: Brookline Books.

Sternberg, R J (1983) 'Criteria for intellectual skills training', *Educational Researcher*, **12**, 6–12.

Sternberg, R J (1985) *Beyond IQ: A triarchic theory of human intelligence*, Cambridge: Cambridge University Press.

Trigwell, K and Prosser, M (1991) 'Relating approaches to study and quality of learning outcomes at the course level', *British Journal of Educational Psychology*, **61**, 265–75.

Van Rossum, E J and Schenk, S M (1984) 'The relationship between learning conception, study strategy and learning', *British Journal of Educational Psychology*, **54**, 73–83.

Volet, S E and Chalmers, D (1992) 'Investigation of qualitative differences in university students' learning goals, based on an unfolding model of stage development', *British Journal of Educational Psychology*, **62**, 17–34.

Vygotsky, L S (1978/1934) *Mind and Society*, Cambridge, Mass: Harvard University Press.

Watkins, D A and Hattie, J (1985) 'A longitudinal study of the approach to learning of Australian tertiary students', *Human Learning*, **4**, 127–42.

Webb, N M (1989) 'Peer interaction and learning in small groups', *International Journal of Educational Research*, **13**, 21–39.

Weinstein, C E (1982) 'A metacurriculum for remediating learning strategies: Deficits in academically underprepared students', in L Noel and R Levitz (eds) *How to Succeed with Academically Underprepared Students*, Iowa City: American College Testing Service National Centre for Advancing Educational Practice.

Weinstein, C E (1988) 'Assessment and training of student learning strategies', in R R Schmeck (ed) *Learning Styles and Learning Strategies*, New York: Putnam.

Weinstein, C E and Meyer, R E (1986) 'The teaching of learning strategies', in M C Wittrock (ed), *Second Handbook of Research on Teaching* (pp.315–26), New York: Macmillan.

Weinstein, C E, Ridley, D S, Dahl, T and Weber, E S (1989) 'Helping students develop strategies for effective learning', *Educational Leadership*, **47**, 17–19.

Wittrock, M C (1990) 'Generative processes of comprehension', *Educational Psychologist*, **24**, 345–76.

Woolfolk, A E (1993) *Educational Psychology* (3rd edn), Boston: Allyn & Bacon.

Index